RAISE YOUR SALES GAME

Play - Win - Rise

FREDERIC R. SAVOYE

TABLE OF CONTENTS

To my father,
Jean-Philippe Savoye

PROLOGUE

S trap in, because you are about to step into the world of sales and business development, a journey that's taken me from humble beginnings to global success over the last thirty years. My career started to accelerate in Bucharest when I took on the role of director of sales and marketing at a well-known high-end hotel, a role I snagged in my ambitious mid-twenties. That job was my ticket to an international career that spanned continents, taking me through Manhattan, Prague, Luxembourg, Cairo, Vienna, and Barcelona, and landing me in the futuristic cityscape of Dubai, where I currently live.

Back in my college days at the University of Sorbonne, studying business and finance, I never dreamed I'd end up in sales or hospitality. However, life is full of surprises, and our choices can have a profound impact on our destiny. That's how a summer job at a three-star hotel in Paris at the age of 19 changed my life, sending me down a path I never expected but wouldn't trade for anything.

This book is for anyone in sales who dreams of making it big, no matter where you are starting from. I'm here to share everything I've learned—from the ground up to the executive level. If you're looking for real, practical advice to skyrocket your career in sales, you've come to the right place. This isn't just my story; it could be the start of yours, too.

Throughout my career, I've seen many colleagues hit a standstill, stuck in the same spot, their roles unchanged for years. Their early enthusiasm has dulled, replaced by disappointment and the inevitable gray hairs of stress. Yet, this isn't what a career in sales should look like. It should be exciting and rewarding, offering self-fulfillment and opportunities to travel, explore global cities, and provide well for your family.

The real goal of this book isn't just to help you do well in your current sales position. It's to equip you with the knowledge and mindset to climb the ranks in the vast sales landscape. It's for those who aim to lead teams, carve out significant roles in large companies, or develop seasoned expertise for personal advancement. This book is your compass to raise your sales game!

It is all about boosting your sales career and personal development. We'll break down how to sharpen your mindset, amp up your communication skills, and polish your personal branding. It's straight talk about getting better at selling and growing as a person. Ready to kick your sales into high gear and find more fulfillment in what you do? Turn this page and jumpstart your journey to success!

CHAPTER 1
BE LUCKY

They say that luck is when opportunity meets preparation. In fact, a lot of people usually attribute the success of high-flyers to pure luck, blaming advantages such as birth with a silver spoon or meeting the right people in the right places. However, I'm here to claim that this so-called "luck" isn't just a matter of chance. This is the result of following some time-honored principles that make the way for many to succeed. These principles are about being on the move and constantly testing the boundaries, which allows us to take opportunities with both hands and to make decisions.

Now, on the other hand, have you ever observed that there are people who never get lucky? Mostly, it means not disturbing the status quo and sticking to what is familiar. Comfort zones are good, but who are we kidding – nothing really important happens there. The big bad wolves of luck are sitting on their haunches, doing nothing and watching others with envy. Wish to outwit them in their own game? It's simple: move, be curious, and continue to challenge. Thus, to avoid the trap of "unluckiness," you have to get down to work, grab the bull by the horns, and hunt for chances by going out of your comfort zone into the wild world of fresh thoughts and views.

You know, being open-minded and interacting with those who think differently can really turn the tide in your favor. Every time you venture into something new or decide to talk to someone who is not part of your usual crowd, you are opening doors to possibilities. Successful people didn't just sit and wait for luck to come to them. They went out, found other points of view, and learned from them. Luck seems to favor those who are constantly on the move, curious, and determined. It is clearly not desirable to sit idle, procrastinating and envying.

Through this process, I have learned not to fear each uphill battle because, in every good stride I take, there is a potential for so many possibilities waiting to be grabbed with courage and a positive attitude. Besides, we enhance our "luck" potential by being distinguished and well-rounded through acquiring new knowledge like crafts or traversing new territories.

My first encounter with the hospitality industry was when the internet was a futuristic concept and the professional packages offered by colleges and universities were not operational. Obtaining knowledge on a specific topic required a true quest, often traveling to libraries or cultural centers to acquire books or CDs. Although the situations we choose to undergo may seem a waste of energy and time initially, they become the key to frequently accessing the golden opportunities awaiting us. Therefore, the time has already come for us. Hence, don't just stay here, expecting luck to come and knock on your door. Instead, react and look for it.

At the age of 19, I chose to spend the summer working at a hotel in Paris, hoping to save more money and show around the city to my English girlfriend. As for my personal experience, the job had me up and about at the crack of dawn, ten-hour shifts five days a week. Giving up my summer was a pretty big sacrifice, but I decided, whatever the cost, it was worth it.

In the hotel, the major task at the reception was to advise the tourists about the places to visit in Paris. However, there was a trick – we were supposed to convince them to take some particular taxis to the airport. Why? Because we get a little kickback from those taxi drivers. They would drop in to shake hands with us, followed by a five or ten-dollar affirmation of gratitude. Frequently, the taxis showed up with the meter already running, meaning that a guest was already paying more than necessary at the beginning of the ride. This entire scenario disturbed me and made me wonder, is this how we are taking advantage of people's trust?

The responsibilities of the work and standing for a long period were challenging for me, too. However, I became determined to learn the software the hotel chain used to accomplish the check-in/check-out, deal with the reservation calls, and ensure the financial backup of the day became in order. At the end of each month, the tips became a frequent source of contention among the front desk team regarding how they were distributed amongst the various employees. Still, it became a way to earn some extra money, so I did not complain and took my due as the others did.

At the end of that summer, the Hotel Director of another small 3-star hotel from the same chain happened to fall into a waterfall in Thailand during his vacation. He could not perform some front desk tasks he was required to accomplish. This left the hotel team short-staffed to operate appropriately, as the entire team initially consisted of only one director (himself), a Front Desk Clerk, one Housekeeping Manager in charge of preparing breakfast, one Bellboy responsible for maintenance, and two Night Auditors to manage a 47-room hotel located in one of the least desirable locations of Paris, near Porte de Montreuil.

The little chain of hotels suddenly needed someone to support the director by performing the tasks of a Front Desk Clerk, for whom he was usually responsible since the team was already the minimum size imaginable. Because of my familiarity with the software, I was offered the job since I was immediately operational and up for the challenge.

Taking this job after the end of my summer vacation was not an uncomplicated choice. It resulted in me waking every weekend at 5 a.m. and crossing the whole of Paris to work 12-hour shifts every Saturday and Sunday. The job was probably the most boring I've had to accomplish: being the Front Desk Clerk of a hotel with a limited inventory that did not reach 10% occupancy on its best days. The only good thing was that there were no tips, so I didn't have to struggle with any problems of conscience.

There were days when the biggest excitement was the fax machine ringing in the tiny back office behind the front desk. I'd run over, hoping that it was the booking coming through, at last, something to do. However, usually, it was just another ad. Even though I was mostly staring at the clock, I learned a lot about patience and how to make the best of a boring day. Weekends turned into months, and I kept my chin up, talking to our regulars and greeting the odd tourist who arrived by bus. However, one scene was repeating itself, and that ended up piquing my curiosity.

An English lady would open the door of a large bus with about 80 people, let a few couples off to check into our place, and then take the rest away. She would return for them at the end of their visit. One day, I plucked up the courage and just had to ask her: "What is the destination of the bus after leaving the hotel?" I was surprised to hear that she took the tourists to a huge 3-star hotel tower where the rest of the group was staying a couple of miles away. It struck me like a flash that if this group were to stay at our hotel instead, we'd be hopping busy!

Once I got the lady's contact, I asked her and her English friends to have Parisian picnics in the city's beautiful parks in spring. I had free time from the university, so I spent a few afternoons on that. It dawned on me at those picnics that snatching their business wasn't rocket science – I just needed to adjust our rates to be more competitive. The management of this business decided to give me a shot, and suddenly, they looked at our hotel as a cute little boutique, a refreshing change from what they were used to. A brief chat with my boss, and before we knew it, our hotel was the next stop for these British groups.

On this wave, I requested more duties, and before I knew it, I was the part-time Sales Manager. This victory enabled us to employ a receptionist who would take over my weekend responsibilities, thus leaving me free to concentrate on catching new clients. In a few months, the director was promoted to Cluster Hotel Director of three properties, and I now became the Cluster Sales Manager of the hotels.

It is a typical "what comes around goes around" story. However, at that time, I didn't really understand that I was building the ground for my career. Without taking a stance on what I believed in and only following what I was interested in, I would not have gotten this chance, which not only made my boss hit his targets but made my job much more fulfilling as I went through my Master's studies in the evening. I was on cloud nine when I got my first business cards, announcing me as a "Cluster Sales Manager" at 20.

Speaking of "luck," I have a few things related to what I said before. Getting that summer job gave me a steady income through my studies. Working in a hotel with no tips and a rather gloomy atmosphere was a challenge not many would have taken. However, by being genuinely curious and seeking ways to improve the standard of our hotel, I put a real dent in my future. Had I not made these choices, I would not have ended my studies with the Sales Manager badge of three hotels. Moreover, it led to the position of key account corporate manager for

SME in the center of Paris after a larger, international group took over our small chain.

Luck, basically, is all about being at the right place at the right time, with the right attitude to grab opportunities. In other words, if you want to be an opportunity for others, it is convenient to be seen as an opportunity yourself.

CHAPTER 2
RAISE YOUR SALES GAME

I n Chapter 1, you acknowledged the role that luck plays in generating business opportunities and the key actions that can impact the odds of being lucky. However, while luck can help get your foot in the door, you need more than luck to close deals. Turning opportunities into actual business requires skill and technique. This is where mastering sales is essential.

Selling isn't just something people wing; it's an art and science that people have perfected for hundreds of years. And yes, while we've got all sorts of tech at our fingertips to learn these skills, I'm a big believer in the old-school approach of learning from those who've been in the trenches: experienced sales coaches. Chapter 1 provided an example of how beginner's luck may have thrown a deal together for a small hotel group series. By mastering sales techniques, you can be certain that your luck and success are really founded on knowledge and skill.

Back in '98, I got lucky again by getting into a top-notch sales training program in Paris. At the time, the company I worked for was bringing on a new sales force, and they wanted to ensure that every field salesperson followed the same protocol. The world champion in photocopier sales, one of the most prestigious references in the business world for sales performance, inspired the training's methodologies.

This tech giant's sales team was constantly pushed to refine their sales techniques. Their strategy involved seeking out new accounts and "farming" existing ones by convincing them to upgrade to the latest, more expensive photocopiers. The pitch often centered on the new models' energy savings and efficiency gains. Though it might seem a weak angle, this approach dominated the industry. The prestige of having the latest model became a source of pride for corporate clients as a symbol of their technological edge.

This top technology company had a smart approach to selling their photocopiers, to sell not only a product but also an idea of a better future at the workplace. They persuaded businesses that buying the newest, although more expensive, model was not just a purchase but an investment in productivity and future savings. The goal was to create a superior work environment with excellent tech support so employees could easily complete their daily activities. Moreover, the sales team communicated the benefits of the photocopier well, even to the customers who already had a good one. They also went further by training the customer's staff to advocate these new photocopiers to their colleagues and bosses. This transformation of employees into brand ambassadors selling photocopiers turned out to be a gold mine.

I am not going to teach in-depth basic sales techniques here, but I would like to emphasize the role of continuous learning and development for sales professionals. If your company provides training opportunities, grab them with enthusiasm. But let's cut to the chase and talk about the skill of posing the right questions. In every sales meeting, the right questions can change everything.

Here's a quick rundown of the types of questions that can help build rapport and significantly boost your chances of closing a deal:

Breaking ice questions: Initiate discussion in a friendly and relaxed atmosphere at the beginning of the meeting.

Open questions: Comprehend the client's needs, issues, and goals.

Probing questions: Prompt a client to acquire more detailed information when the rapport is on.

Confirmation questions: Receive affirmative answers from the client, for instance, "yes."

Agreement questions: Assist the client in recognizing the value and benefits of your solution in meeting their needs and moving toward closing the deal.

In the sales world, building value in the customer's eyes is a crucial part of the sales process. One effective way to achieve this is by creating an environment that gives the client the perception that they are making a bargain. For instance, if you are a salesperson, let your customer believe that you fought hard internally on their behalf to get them a special discount, even if you could have given it to them on the spot. This strategy creates a sense of exclusivity for the customer, thereby increasing the perceived value they see in your product or solution.

Take the example of the global giant in photocopiers. They provided their sales team with the information to demonstrate how much more efficient their new machines were, assuring substantial energy savings—even to those who owned pretty good photocopiers. The sales representatives were trained to teach the account employees how to sell internally to their colleagues and superiors. This approach ultimately resulted in the company's dominance as a leader in the photocopier industry.

Last, but not least, it is a critical skill to identify some hidden needs that even the decision-maker is unaware of. Mastering this ability sets a brilliant sales professional apart from the rest.

By adequately qualifying the account and understanding the client's motivations in-depth, a salesperson can uncover these hidden needs and present them to the client as an opportunity to solve a problem they were unaware of. This skill can be the key to closing a deal, as the salesperson suddenly becomes the only one proposing a solution that goes beyond the client's initial expectations. Such an approach allows the sales professional to make a difference and close the deal. To illustrate this, I would like to share a story from the Czech Republic in 2004.

Upon arriving in Prague to oversee the commercialization of seven properties, I was surprised, when analyzing a report, to find out that a big international shipping company had been booking thousands of rooms in two 4-star hotels of our competition. Out of curiosity, I reached out to the Prague-based travel agency in charge of the travel arrangements for the shipping company.

It made me to directly reach the person responsible for the regional department near Prague, only 10 km from the downtown.

A visit to his office a few days later allowed me to qualify for the business opportunity. The company was restructuring its global logistics, and Prague was chosen as the new European headquarters location. This project could significantly impact one of my hotels, located just a couple of miles away from the hotels they were currently using. However, the client had one major concern: A bridge separated my hotel's location from their current preferred location, and the route was infamous for its daily traffic jams at the beginning and end of every working day. His guests staying at my property would lose significant time on the daily commute, going back and forth.

During our initial meeting, the decision-maker let me know that he would not consider a hotel such as mine if it were located on this side of the bridge. It appeared to be the deal killer. I didn't give up. Our relationship continued. I invited him to some of our golf events because he was a passionate golfer. I thought it would be a good way for him to enjoy golf, the company of our community's key business decision-makers, and try and break out of what appeared to be an impasse.

I glimpsed a ray of light when I used the data analysis to be listed on their preferred list. I noticed that during the busiest time, the city's hotels were full, and their guests had to pay rack rates at any available hotels at that time, including mine. It was a nice incentive for them to start considering my hotel as one of the official vendors and have them benefit from a special rate. Nevertheless, this situation led to my property being seen as just a backup option, something to fall back on only when the rest of the city was fully booked. My hotel was a standby hotel for high occupancy periods, and that was just like a bitter pill to swallow for me and wasn't a success.

The fact that the shipping company had not booked any room yet could be considered a failure. Still, we were granted an opportunity thanks to our participation in the hotel program: A few weeks later, during a business trip, I got the chance to visit another travel agency that handled the account from the U.K. During a friendly chat with the agency manager, I brought up a question about what problems the Prague-based decision-maker was facing with their mega project.

To my surprise, she mentioned that he frequently complained about the enormous expense reports his consultants were submitting. They were all taking taxis to work, even the top-tier consultants staying in luxury hotels in the old town's center. Expenses were skyrocketing mainly because of the severe traffic jams during peak hours. This piece of information was a revelation for me. I couldn't wait to get back to Prague, now feeling really optimistic about cracking the account, convinced that success was just around the corner.

The second time I dropped into his office out of the city, the decision maker was curious when he saw me without any prior notification. "Fred, what brings you here again?" he asked. I presented him with some branded golf balls, hoping they would be enough to make peace, and with a smile, I said, "I think it is about time that we discuss a resolution for our partnership."

Smiling, he joked, "Did you finally move your hotel to the other side of the bridge?" I laughed off the joke, saying, "Not quite. However, what if I told you that your consultants' costs in Prague could be cut down by choosing my hotel instead?"

He was certainly interested in what I had to say. "How is that possible?" he asked.

I handed him an envelope with his company's logo, saying, "Inside is a 'Travel Kit' for guests staying at my hotel," I explained. "It includes step-by-step instructions, complete with pictures, on how to take the metro from my hotel to your facilities within twenty minutes, door to door. And, of course, it also comes with free metro tickets for the trip."

Upon opening the envelope and reading the instructions, his attitude changed. "This could work and solve a big issue I have!" he agreed. "Let me instruct the travel department to put your hotel on the first place of the list for our consultants as I really like the idea, Fred," he said.

My hotel had been the most preferred for the company's consultants within a few months after this discussion, generating around 500 thousand dollars in sales. The account became the second biggest for our property, and it all began with a simple strategy, a simple idea of making it cheaper and easier for them to go to the office.

The shipping account story illustrates identifying and satisfying the customer's hidden needs, which is the key to sales differentiation. Selling a product or service is not only about selling a product or service; it is also about understanding their unique pain points and tailoring a solution just for them.

But it's not all about making sales. These skills are crucial in leadership positions, too. Organizations are on the hunt for leaders who can not only drive growth but also build lasting relationships with clients and be decisive. Being adept at sales techniques and understanding the needs of both your team and your clients can make all the difference. So, whether you're aiming to move up within your current company or gearing up for a new role elsewhere, refining these abilities can be a major factor in your success. By getting better at sales, making strong bonds with clients, and deeply understanding what they're after, you can position yourself as a valuable asset to any organization.

CHAPTER 3
PERCEPTION IS KEY

The previous section discussed the importance of selling techniques in success. Further, it is essential to comprehend the role of creating a suitable setting for closing great deals. However, it's crucial to lay the groundwork for success in sales, especially when it comes to accounts that could potentially be game-changers for your organization. The necessity that every account gets a fair share of attention is vital. Still, the most important aspect is prioritizing those that could have a significant impact on your company when fully activated. By deftly working through these critical major accounts, you are in a solid position to set yourself apart as decisive in your organization and move closer to your professional dreams in the sector.

In this chapter, we'll elaborate on how to create a favorable environment and take full advantage of the opportunities that, sooner or later, start appearing as a recurring reward for persistent sales pros. Let's now go through some high-level approaches to take your sales game to the next level and achieve your goals!

It often appears that in the world of sales, you spend all your time convincing potential customers that investing in your product or service is worthwhile. This usually leads to the negative loop of adjusting the prices to close the deal. True professionals know the key to successful sales is a mindset shift that starts with not convincing the buyer but rather creating a scenario where they think they need the product more than sales reps want their business. Sealing the deal with the only argument that you're the most inexpensive option in the market is not sustainable and is a telltale sign that essential skills are missing.

Instead of always figuring out how to sell your product at a bargain, smartly managing the time factor can make all the difference. Often, the price may not even be what the buyer cares most about and is just a way to put you off. So, to set the discussion in such a way that a buyer would be actively looking to close a deal with you, you have to be strategic about your timing to increase the value perception of your product.

To clarify this, let me provide a personal story highlighting the crucial role of timing in sales. As a teenager, I dated the daughter of a very successful CEO of a well-known Paris-based communications company. He often shared some of his experiences as a young creative director of a company he eventually sold for millions of dollars a few years later.

He gave me an example of an important meeting he had attended when his company was pitching a huge national media campaign for a new soda product in the French market. The contract was valued at millions of French francs, and winning it could make the company financially solid for many years.

During the introductory meeting, the CEO, being a young creative at that time, interrupted the proceedings and proposed a great idea for the main campaign slogan and went on to develop its following variations. The decision maker heard the idea but treated it as a small case and paid no real attention to the concept presented to him. When the meeting came to an end, the young creative's senior associate was angry at him because he disclosed the idea too soon. He explained that revealing the motto he had in mind in the meeting prematurely disclosed the company's most valuable asset: a detailed idea to be promoted, carefully presented with the right timing.

Now, what he should have done (even if the story was ending the same way) was to treat it as if they had developed the concept after a few weeks of intensive work because this would have really made the client believe that a full team behind it did a lot. And this was enough to justify letting it have the high price they could charge for service delivery. Therefore, the creation of the concept for the campaign had to be started from scratch, as the idea was not introduced at the right time to be considered relevant enough. During that dinner, the soon-to-be CEO learned an important lesson about the significant role of timing and perception in sales and marketing, which he passed on to me.

The CEO's senior associate stated that premature disclosure of the company's most valuable asset— an elaborated concept in this case—could result in the client not considering the product or service as valuable enough to pay a high price. His lesson is not only applicable to the intellectual assets of a company, such as ideas and concepts but to all types of products and services that need strategic timing in sales and marketing. The concept is also illustrated in the following story.

In a typical hospitality scenario, you can often see sales representatives positioning themselves as defenders of the client's interests rather than those of the hotels that employ them. This holds true even when they are tooting the horns of their own hotels for which they are fighting the cause. For example, a sales representative of a hotel group tasked with including luxury hotels in a high-end agency network is responsible for ensuring that a maximum number of his hotels are featured in their selection. The goal is to attract the most elite clientele that such a consortium brings together. However, what one finds on the factory floors is not the perfect scenario these sales directors sometimes deliver.

I've had situations in which sales representatives justify these luxury hotel network decision-makers as to why they should not consider certain of their hotels for inclusion in their portfolio. Without noticing, they slip into the role of a consultant company for their client instead of their own team, forgetting who feeds and pays their bills. In certain cases, these representatives will act, only avoiding shooting themselves in the foot, to earn the trust of the networks with whom they are partnered, no matter what it takes, perhaps even giving away their own hotels in the process. Although this strategy smoothed their relations with the account reps, it damaged their main mission of adding hotels to the list of coveted networks and signing agreements, as their devotion to the customer superseded their loyalty to their company. Furthermore, they lost potential opportunities and didn't reach their goal of expanding business significantly with their clients.

Moreover, in my experience of being in sales pitches in different regions across the globe, I have seen that hotel buyers will often fall for that salesperson who wears a consultant's hat with sincerity. The demands of the buyers increased, too, since they wanted a single person to be their point of contact in the hotel chain. This renowned sales director would have communicated with them for years to their benefit. This situation was profit-destructive as important accounts often ended up being handled by people who put the relationship with the client ahead, harming the hotels they were meant to support.

At first sight, you might think this approach is a stroke of genius for the hotel chains wanting to build solid relationships with buyers, but the reality was quite a different story for the hotel's profits. It was a win-win for the "consultant" sales directors and their clients – both sides were putting themselves on the back, with the sales directors feeling like the belle of the ball, the go-to person for their clients. The other side of the coin was that the client was in a comfortable seat, knowing that there would not be much of a hassle to get the best deals and that there would be no pressure to include additional hotels as a counterpart. Moreover, all this was because of the sales representative who was ready to do anything to keep the relationship by ensuring that they constantly secured top-notch offers for what became their friend. Of course, this arrangement was not a money-making machine for the hotels.

Having seen this pattern repeatedly and feeling inspired, I knew that it was high time to make a change and take a different path with my sales team. Believe me. It was not only a great success but also a lot of fun for us to formulate our strategy and refine our approach to the big fish. Our plan was straightforward but brilliant: We decided to play the part of the naïve sales representative, cheeky enough to throw a little bit of shade at our superiors and act as if there was some sort of battle going on behind the scenes – all in an effort to lock in rates that we sold to our clients as the deal of the century.

I led my team to stage a small play for our clients. For instance, I recommended they inform the client that they had bent over backward to schedule an appointment with the regional director of sales and the hotel's general manager in order to negotiate the lowest possible rate to finalize the deal. As per our script, the general manager was to take a tough stance and reject the rates as being too low, almost at cost. Then, the sales representative would leave the clients with a little baiting, saying they'd be back by the end of the day, hoping the supreme meeting of all the top bosses would work for them.

At the end of the day, a message would be sent to the client by the sales manager, which would be a spin yarn about the general manager digging in their heels, and now a call is being made in the evening, with the vice president of operations being brought into the call in a last-ditch effort to close the deal for the benefit of the client. They'd assure to keep the clients updated on the outcome first thing the day after. By morning, the clients would be offered the normal entry rate – no additional discounts – presented as the aftermath of world battles fought against the management in reality, not an actual battle. The agreement would be, as expected, struck at that time.

Yes, this approach was quite borderline, but the results were amazing. The team had a blast with it, getting more and more bold in their sales approaches and scoring some truly incredible successes. The icing on the cake? Everyone ended up happy. The clients believed that they got a fantastic deal without realizing that they had paid a fair price. Moreover, this satisfied the general manager as the profitability ensured that they received the best service. This way, the client's business was secured, and loyalty was maintained for the long run.

In concluding this chapter, it's essential to highlight that creating an environment conducive to sales is crucial for success in any industry. It doesn't matter if you are selling a physical product, a service, or an idea; the manner in which you present it to buyers can meaningfully affect the value they place on the product or service. Skipping this step in the sales process leaves the salesperson fighting an uphill battle to close deals at any price. The result is invariably a sales performance that leaves much to be desired. That's not the desired outcome for someone committed to excelling and becoming recognized as a top professional in their field.

This book is not only about becoming a better salesperson but also a guide to reaching the level of top executives sooner than you imagined. To reach this goal, no matter what field you work in, it's important to make a difference by spending time creating the right setting for successful sales when you're working with buyers.

CHAPTER 4
FIND THE HIDDEN NEED

To do well in sales, it's key to set the standard so buyers see what you have to offer in the best light. This is a stepping stone to success. Yet, I truly believe we can stand head and shoulders above our competitors by sharpening a specific talent. If you can perfect it, it will allow you to build a strong relationship between you, as the sales professional, and your buyers, making a critical and positive impact in a competitive market.

My approach is focused on making sure that you and your product aren't just involved in the market but that you truly stand out, going beyond the mere transaction of goods for money. This is the opportunity for you to interact with the buyer in ways that most salespeople neglect by satisfying needs that they might not even be aware that they have. I call these "hidden needs," and when these are fulfilled, the deal is almost done. This is not a matter of pricing others out; this is about creating bindings that are not easily severed.

Handling buyers is all about putting yourself in their shoes and understanding their unsaid needs throughout the sales process. Recognizing these needs and offering a relevant solution elevates your offer way above the rest. For instance, let me start with a simple example to get into the idea before moving to a more elaborate scenario.

The world of hotels is full of properties that offer large meeting rooms with all the latest technology and high-quality finishes, which is a standard feature. However, let's be real: who hasn't been from hotel to hotel listening to pitch after the pitch? Picture it: a sales representative singing praises about room sizes, capacities, the many breakout rooms, the flood of natural light, and ballroom ceilings. Ultimately, the job is to sort out the possibilities and strike the best deal possible, especially if your event falls in the off-peak season. Yet, when you finally manage to bring the rates to the ground, there is one sales representative who is so proud because he has managed to close a deal at the lowest price when all the options on the table look basically the same.

In the case of such a scenario, I would not enumerate all the characteristics of my product. Still, after the full qualification of the requirements, I would show what in my product would be only ticked by the buyer in terms of what is required. Rather, I would like to take advantage of the time I spend with the client to form a solid rapport and to learn about the objective of the meeting and the personal commitment level to the project they are commissioned to source and organize.

I would pose my questions to the decision maker to show them that this project they are working on is a real opportunity to make it a smashing success and an opportunity to shine in front of their organization. For instance, I would ask the pedigree of the people at that meeting, who is organizing it, and the purpose of the meeting.

I would make sure we arrive at the importance of this meeting to be successful since the budget allocated for it is significant, and I would admit the chance or the risk the buyer is going to take by managing such a strategic project. This method is not only about getting your event done and dusted but rather working together to ensure that your event is memorable and everyone leaves with more than they expected.

Further, it is equally essential to give a client the opportunity to escape embarrassment or be applauded, informing them that the outcome is hinged on their performance. I am usually thankful to tell them that I actually understand the significance of what is at hand when it comes to the organization of such an event. Here, I assure them that I will be the one to personally and closely supervise the event's success, which implies to them that they are on the safe side with me since I will make this event glowing in their organization.

This approach, when communicated effectively, resonates deeply with many employees' aspirations: aspiration and the desire for a life that brings forth new possibilities and opportunities for development as well as potential new professional opportunities. Picking you and nobody else to do business with could simply answer this need far beyond just organizing a meeting on behalf of their company.

To back this up, I am going to tell you about my own

experience in Prague in 2006. Keeping the preceding in mind, I used market data, which is easily accessible to the hotel industry, and discovered a pattern in bookings from Italy to the city's largest hotel, an 800-room behemoth located just a few minutes' drive from one of my 4-star boutique hotels. This intrigued me, and after doing more research, I learned that these bookings were made by a prominent Italian bank as it underwent a merger with the largest national bank of the Czech Republic. This merger was a grand project for information technology (I.T.) integration between the two entities and was undoubtedly on the way to become the largest account in the city.

My approach was mainly done in two ways:

First, I asked one of my well-trained sales managers to contact the buyer and do whatever it took to build the relationship, as we'd need them to give us the opportunity to propose our 4-star hotel when the time came. She did, and she nailed securing a dinner with the lady in charge of hotel sourcing. That dinner ran into the early hours, and I gave a day off to my team member the day after, as the wine in Prague can be very strong, and the main objective had been accomplished: they were now both best friends when in town.

This resulted in a request to the sales manager, a couple of weeks later, to go on a trip to Milan to spend a couple of days shopping with the decision-maker. The trip was approved and sponsored by my company. Although the buyer was very enthusiastic about our friendly and original approach, she did not see any immediate reason to move from her current arrangement, which provided a very competitive rate of 95 euros for bed and breakfast at the city's number one 5-star hotel.

In parallel and as a second step, I analyzed the account's booking patterns, looking at the data for clues. In the winter months, the Italian bank always received a flat rate of 95 euros, showing the loyalty of their favorite hotel, which honored the contracted rate. Yet, an interesting finding was recorded for May, the high tourist season in Prague. The average rate paid by the bank's employees soared above 200 Euro, thereby indicating that the hotel of their choice was focusing on more lucrative segments rather than on the bank's guests who had to look for other 5-star hotels at the current rates with no discounts.

This finding exposed the decision maker's undelivered requirement of a constant and dependable booking experience, unaltered by the seasonal rate fluctuation. Having noticed this, I asked my sales manager to communicate this information to the buyer, stating that the policy of their preferred hotel had put them in bad condition during the high season, which resulted in increased costs and logistical challenges for their employees dispersed around Prague. This approach not only showed our deep understanding of the buyer's situation but also set our boutique hotel as a dependable and attentive option able to meet their real needs.

After agreeing that the current booking situation was absolutely unacceptable, I had my sales manager offer a clever solution: For their major project that was starting in Prague, which was taking up thousands of room nights, we would set 90 Euro per night as the rate at our four-star boutique hotel, just a stone's throw away from their usual five-star place. We pledged to observe this rate for any stay at our Prague hotels, even offering it to our three-star properties. And if visitors landed at a three-star, we would foot the bill for their taxi to the office.

Presenting a better and guaranteed rate, regardless of the hotel's star ranking, was the ticket. This account ended up producing a little over twenty thousand rooms and nights per year for a three-year term. We actually overfilled my hotel's portfolio since most of the time, we were simply sending all of the bookings to our 3-star property, where the guests had to pay €90 vs. about €50, which interestingly was the rate published on these budget hotels' signs. This approach shot up the performance of our hotels to unprecedented levels. In less than six months, I was ascending the ladder to the position of vice president of sales, marketing, and revenue for the luxury segment of our hotel group. By 35, I was getting one of the highest salaries in the sales division and managing a proud portfolio of hotels from London to Moscow.

Others may regard it as a fluke — having arrived at the right time and place, with the right information and the best team. And they would be right. Nevertheless, luck is not something that comes from the sky. It's all about focusing on the goal and doing everything in your power to achieve it. Some will argue that this success is industry-specific to hospitality. However, talking to sales professionals from different industries revealed to me that this approach could work in any place. I will substantiate it with a digression from my hospitality career when I was 26. Sure that my future lay outside my native land,

I quit a good job in Paris to travel to other places. I came to the U.S. to begin anew and took a job with the largest privately-held rental car company just outside Washington, DC.

CHAPTER 5
CHANGING TERRITORY

At the beginning of the summer of 1998, I benefited from my first annual review as a key account manager in Paris. After a fantastic success story the past year, I had to ask about the opportunities I could grasp in the year ahead and to stay on the path with energy and endurance! I was at a fork in the road, and the idea was to leave abroad, possibly relocate in the next few months, commence an expat phase in this international hotel group, and travel the world.

Considering my position in this company and the positive feedback on my work, it was a natural response to the question asked by the assessor of how I saw my future, simply by leveraging internal opportunities abroad. But the answer I got was in a diplomatic manner; it was a matter of the fact that since I was doing well in my current position, I should stay there. I was told to enjoy my small annual salary raise, consider myself lucky, and go on as I was for the next 4-5 years before even thinking about the possibility of working abroad—a possibility they implied would grow or fade with time.

This perspective was disheartening. The idea of progressing only in the usual way to become an area sales director, as if it were the highest achievement, felt constricting. The role, though respectable, looked like a guarantee of monotony and boredom, which was so remote from the dynamic career development I pictured. From this perspective, promotion to area director of sales looked a long way with little strategic value, probably side-lining any aspirations for broader career development until my mid-30s.

This awareness sparked an inner dialogue about finding an alternative to the typical middle-class Parisian life—managing a small team of account managers in a few districts of a big French city only to eventually find myself trapped in a draining lifestyle and accepting an endless cycle of "commute, work, sleep." Despite being portrayed by the media as the ideal of success, this life felt unsatisfying. Indeed, the dominant storyline broadcasted in Paris by the media at that time was that getting a full-time job was proof of being successful in life, and that was it.

1998 was also the birth of the internet age. It really wasn't too long before fax machines gave way to emails, and the dot-com phenomenon was born. In those days, just loading a simple webpage was torture of patience, and the hot news was that some U.S. universities included books and artistic content on their web pages that were made available to all. Magazines of the time would have lists of web addresses, which invited readers to a digital adventure in an era when Google didn't even exist.

After that yearly assessment, the way ahead of me was

evident, not the one I wanted to take. The dilemma was to find a new direction to take me away from the ordinary and into something new and developing. The findings from my annual review made me curious about stepping out of my comfort zone. That's why every day at about 8 p.m. I started surfing the net, searching for job applications, and trying to open as many doors as possible. However, I didn't know the outcome. I noticed that the longer I was in Paris, the more I felt like I was going around in circles.

Even though I was considered one of the shining stars of my sector, I felt that I could have been less competitive than other excellent people in the entire industry. I was sure that it was my time to get rid of shyness and become fluent in English, but in what way—it was a real puzzle. My resolve, however, was unwavering: I was determined that I would be the one to create the needed opportunities for myself. At that time, it was a hard task.

While in the past, job announcements were published in the weekly print newspapers. It took me entire afternoons to write hundreds of handwritten letters along with my most recent CV – a process that was quite exhausting. The outcome of the efforts that I made was very disorienting, to put it mildly, and I went back at the same time to post my resume on online job sites randomly. I went through the early internet on search engines like altavista.com, which was the ruler in the digital era back then. I typed in the keywords with no specific expectations, and this was the same as throwing a note in a bottle into an immense ocean of the virtual world, where one cannot be sure of achieving something concrete.

At last, my direct superior at that time had the opportunity to move to another position in the group, nearer to where she lived, and was replaced by a young and ambitious executive. It didn't take long for him to make his stance clear: he perceived me as his rival who had to be controlled right away. I felt like I was living in a workplace where a cold wind blew through every day, and I had to balance my life on a tightrope.

To escape this everyday tensed-up negative atmosphere in the office, I would have organized dinner parties for my friends at home. But what had been my surprise, I got a phone call I didn't expect. And then, the voice on the other end, speaking in English, gave me the news—I was invited for an interview for a job I had applied online some time ago. My English was pretty shaky at that time. Thus, I couldn't grasp any details, not even the name of the company. I barely understood that the mail would contain the rest of the information.

Keeping their promise, an official invite arrived in my mailbox a few days later, making me realize that I should start improving my English on a fast track. Having only one week to get ready, this was the opportunity for me to escape from the Parisian rat race, maybe my only chance for a long time. Resolute, I bought a set of 4 CDs called "Learn How to Speak Business English" and plunged into learning. I stuffed as many handy phrases and idioms as I could, hoping to equip myself for what might be the interview of my life.

That day of the interview, I was led into an unusual setting, a huge ballroom full of more than a hundred people who came with a mix of curiosity and expectation. I managed to get a spot among the crowd, and in no time, the event started. A group of American assessors came up on the stage, and their presentation was displayed on the big screen. They presented their organization, which was a leading player in the car rental industry, with plans to expand in France. They were here in Paris to scout talent for their future management team, offering a golden ticket: a selected few would fly to the U.S. for 18 months to get involved in the business before returning to France to head new branches. This company, they bragged, was the biggest of its kind in the U.S., a family-owned empire.

The process of selection was a smooth-running engine. We were split into groups of 20-30, going through a set of tests that were supposed to demonstrate our capabilities. One second, I was having a small talk with my colleague candidate, and the next, I was given a minute to sell him to the audience on why he should be the chosen one. Another problem we had to discuss was the launch of a new car rental branch, determining the perfect location. The underlying purpose was evident – to identify those of us who would not only be able to start a conversation but also to engage others, coming forward as leaders.

This specific test was a crucible of persuasion and assertiveness. I had to hold my group's attention, with direct eye contact, and lead the conversation, having to anticipate who might take the lead. Although my English was not flawless, a combination of determination and adrenaline pushed me to lead the discussion. True, the struggle with the limited vocabulary and shaky grammar was daunting, but it did not prevent me. I never lost my concentration. Moreover, in some way, I was the leader of the pack, maneuvering through my language obstacles with a mix of determination and spur-of-the-moment resourcefulness.

Following those first obstacles, the evaluators had a short break, and we had to wait in suspense for our destiny for what seemed like forever. However, in reality, it was just a half an hour. On their return, the air became charged as they began to reject most of the gathered hopefuls. Only twenty of us were retained, and I was one of them. I felt a mixture of pride and excitement.

The last obstacle was a personal interview, where an applicant had a face-to-face meeting with one of the evaluators. Upon stepping into the room, one of the assessors addressed me by my name for the first time, a little act that put the entire situation at ease. She gave me a pen and dared me to sell it to her. This task suited me well as a well-experienced Sales Manager. I resorted to my training, asking open questions to draw out what she wanted and highlighting the pen's unique selling points, pushing a strong case for why this was a pen she couldn't walk away from.

Though my English was limited, armed with a few phrases I'd learned in a crash course I'd recently taken, her smile comforted me. "Frederic, aren't you a sales professional?" she asked, acknowledging my hard work and ability. The moment of recognition was particularly sweet.

When I left that intense afternoon, the assessor thanked me and told me they would keep me informed, adding that they would only take four candidates from France. I left with my chin up but completely aware of my linguistic deficiencies and how they might influence my dreams of a global career.

A couple of days later, I got a call—it was not the news I had been waiting for. They let me know I was on a reserve, the next in line if any of the selected applicants would not confirm their participation in this management program. Disappointed but reflective on where I was lacking, I continued with work, eagerly awaiting my three weeks' vacation to the Caribbean. The break was an opportunity for reflection and recharging, to return to tackle the coming challenges with new eyes.

September 1998 is still a live memory of me stuck in the Paris traffic on a typical Monday morning. The vacation's sweet relief was over, and I was thrown back into the struggle of reality. The schedule for the day was to attend a weekly meeting in a hotel that had been recently acquired by our group, located somewhere in the northern part of the city, a place that I had yet to find on a map since GPS technology didn't still exist. The trip was a high-stakes slalom, with me trying to avoid all the morning delivery trucks and garbage collectors in my trusty Volkswagen Polo, each turn a deliberate attempt to cut off a few seconds of my arrival time.

I was glad that the consequences of my traffic navigation were not as harsh as I had expected. I was only five minutes late and hoped the coffee break had not yet finished. This would have been the ideal time to relax and tell stories of my urban morning adventure with colleagues before getting into the real meat of our meeting. The silence that greeted me in the public areas of the hotel was a loud sign that the meeting had started without me. When I entered the conference room, I felt the chill of disapproval. However, six colleagues, who were already engaged in a heated discussion around the table, did not help to create a welcoming atmosphere.

My arrival appeared to turn on a switch in our new boss, who started to scold me in a way that took me back to my school days; he chastised me for my lateness like I was a rebellious teenager. It was a hard fact to accept that he demanded instant compliance with his rulebook. I sat down amid my colleagues, a whirlwind of anger growing inside as I realized that I would have to work under someone more concerned about proving to his team that he was dominant than anything else. The working day finally ended. Moreover, the journey home brought no relief with the rush hour in Paris, ending a day of trials both in and out of the office.

The day that had started on the wrong foot felt more like a post-vacation nightmare. However, it took an unexpected turn when I stepped back into my apartment. To my surprise, I found an envelope on the floor. I could hardly believe the words in front of me once I opened it. The US-based company I had randomly applied to had chosen me to join their ranks in the Washington, DC, area, starting in early October. The gloom of the day's earlier frustrations suddenly disappeared, replaced by a burgeoning excitement for what comes ahead.

I couldn't wait the following morning to talk with the person who, until that moment, I had considered my boss for the foreseeable future. Anticipation filled the air as he, no doubt, was expecting to continue where we had left off, ready to lecture me on punctuality and discipline. Yet, the conversation that unfolded was nothing like he had anticipated. With a few simple sentences, I let him know about my departure, blowing away any plans he had of molding me further under his stringent management style. The technical knockout quickly followed because he had just been partially responsible for the resignation of his team's best-performing salesperson. I just couldn't hide my pleasure in seeing him widen his eyes while appearing to be in a panic at the time.

CHAPTER 6
WELCOME TO THE USA

J ust a few days after I touched down in Washington, DC, I found myself at a rental car agency in Maryland, one of many in the area. This company was buzzing and clearly on the rise, and it was all thanks to the brilliant idea of the person who started it all. Years back, the visionary owner figured out that a lot of people who need to rent a car can't easily get to the rental place to pick it up. So, what did he do? He came up with a complimentary pick-up service for his customers. This smart move really made the company standout, especially back in the days when finding an affordable taxi ride in the smaller towns was a real headache.

The setup was pretty straightforward: the founder and his son owned all the cars, and they played their cards right by letting customers drop off their rentals at any branch across the country. They didn't stop there, though. Furthermore, the company smartly partnered with car dealerships and body shops, identifying a niche market of customers needing a temporary ride due to car repairs or car accidents.

The branches were nothing fancy—simple setups with white walls, a few desks on grey carpeting, and a spot for complimentary American coffee, the only luxury offered to clients and employees. The staff's daily routine was straightforward: promptly answer calls, pick up clients in need, quickly handle the paperwork back at the office, and try to upsell an upgrade or insurance. Though most of the time, they were already covered.

After the hustle of check-ins and check-outs, we'd give the cars a quick once-over and clean them up for the next round. Every now and then, we'd get to break the monotony by delivering a car to another branch that needed it more—a welcome escape from the long hours that stretched from dawn till dusk, six days a week. Employees were compensated hourly, with the option for overtime to pad their earnings. The real perk, however, was the two weeks of paid vacation, offering a golden opportunity for some well-deserved rest and reflection!

As for career growth, the company's rapid expansion meant constant openings for new roles, especially with the ambition to maintain a rental fleet utilization rate of over 95% across a network that spanned the U.S. and Canada. The goal was clear: once a branch hit the target with a fleet of around 200 units, it was time to scout for a new location to serve even more customers. Starting as an assistant manager and moving up to a manager assistant (despite the titles sounding almost interchangeable), the path led to becoming a branch manager. From there, the sky was the limit, with a shot at managing a cluster of branches and eventually becoming one of the many regional chiefs calling the shots.

Landing in this role was a real eye-opener for me, a young go-getter hungry for opportunities after months and years of repeating the same routine in Paris. Imagine my surprise when I saw how the team, dressed to the nines in white shirts and jackets, took pride in their work. They approached each day with enthusiasm, almost as if they owned the place themselves. This was a far cry from the French attitude I was used to, where scepticism and negativity toward work are more common. Here in the U.S., the vibe was different; the young people were all in, believing fully in the company's philosophy and dreaming big about their futures.

However, it wasn't all sunshine and rainbows. There was a stark contrast I couldn't ignore: retired men, having spent their lives in hard labor, were still working as drivers tirelessly just to make ends meet. Their situation served as a stark reminder of the harsh realities that people face, such as low pensions after years of hard work. But for me, this job was a chance to have a new adventure and experience a new environment. I threw myself into the work, determined to excel at upselling and tackling challenges head-on. While others might shy away from selling insurance that most clients declined, I saw it as a puzzle to solve, a skill to master. My English improved leaps and bounds out of sheer necessity because there was no other option.

I accepted every task, whether cleaning cars until they sparkled or building rapport with the people at the car dealership and the car body shop. My goal was to rent out every single car in the fleet daily. If any were left, I'd drive them to another branch that needed them. I was turning every customer pick-up into a chance to improve my sales skills. Every day brought a new lesson, and I was there to learn it all. And it paid off. Before long, my sales techniques were solid.

The primary focus of the firm's marketing campaign was to introduce an entry rate of $9.99 per day, private pick-up included. The car you got for such a price was the smallest you could ever think of; it was overused and without any options. Also, this car was probably available in 5 of the 200 car average branches, and the customer had to be persistent and strategic to finish renting such a vehicle. For visitors who came for service or car accident, their insurance allowed them to reserve a mid-size model similar to a Toyota Corolla, which would be leased for USD 29,99 a day.

While most of my colleagues were going to pick up the clients with the car for which they booked, I was picking up the best car that was in the parking lot at the time, for example, the Cadillac Escalade, the Dodge Durango or a Chevy Impala if available. As the client got in the car, I got into a conversation quickly, and we discussed everything on our way back to the office. I was using questions to approach the topic of great cars in America, how great the car I was driving was, usually getting a "yes" to the question, "Would you like to try it as it would be quite an experience in comparison to the car you own." Or a "no" when asking, "This Dodge Durango is, in my opinion, the best car we have. I love driving it when picking up my customers. The V8 is so powerful that it feels so awesome when accelerating. I don't feel this way even when driving my own Suzuki Samurai. Have you driven such an SUV before?"

Right off the bat, when guests started chatting with me, I bet they didn't even guess I was aiming to upsell them by the time we wrapped up their rental. They probably thought, "Here's a young international student. He sounds French, probably just driving around to brush up on his English while on a study break." That's how our conversations kicked off: easy and open, all the way to the rental agency. Then, as they stepped out of the car, looking a bit puzzled in the parking lot about where to head next, they seemed genuinely thankful when I guided them into the office.

Imagine their look when I, the guy they thought was just the driver, invited them to sit down at the desk, where I then switched hats and started the official paperwork for their rental. On our way back to the rental branch, I loved getting into conversations with the guests about the car we were in or hearing about the dream car they wished to own someday. This talk helped me gauge how excited they were about cars in general.

If I noticed they were really into the conversation, I'd quickly suggest a deal to them. I'd offer them to rent a fancier, more expensive car than they originally booked at a big discount. This meant they could drive a much better car for just an extra 20 to 30 dollars a day. This approach often worked, and guests were happy to pay more for the experience. Their eyes would light up at the offer, especially if the rental was for a bit of an adventure, like a road trip to another state, so they'd jump at the chance to drive off in style without breaking the bank. It was a win-win, really. They got a slice of luxury at a bargain, and I got the satisfaction of the upsell.

But I wasn't done yet. Next, I'd bring up the idea of insurance, pitching it as a no-brainer to dodge any worries about handling an expensive car. "Why not avoid the headache and potential hit to your wallet if something goes sideways?" I'd suggest. Getting this pitch just right was my main motivation when waking up in the morning. My goal was to find the perfect words, tone, and even facial expressions to make this seem like the deal of the century. In addition, the rest of the job had moments of feeling like Groundhog Day—same stuff, different day, and could be downright tiring. But nailing the upsell? That was where I found my little slice of excitement. Being the go-to guy for insurance and premium rentals didn't pad my pockets directly, but it sure did add a bit of spice to the daily routine. These moments of victory, small as they might be, make all the difference.

It took a good few months to really get the hang of the sales pitch, to the point where I became pretty effective at it. Before I knew it, I was being recognized as one of the top sellers of insurance, often convincing customers to upgrade from the usual $29.99 rental to a $49.99 one, and even adding full coverage at $29.99, which, to be honest, they probably didn't need. The real pat on the back came when, by the end of 1999, I found myself named the best insurance seller in both Virginia and Maryland. This sparked a real competitive spirit among my colleagues, all eager to figure out how a young guy from France was shattering sales records. It even led to some colleagues being temporarily reassigned to my branch just to watch and learn from my technique.

But as the thrill of upselling began to wane, I found myself craving a change. More than a year of repeating the same tasks began to drain my enthusiasm. I didn't see any close changes on the horizon in my journey in the U.S. Moreover, I found myself longing for a new direction, something to reignite my passion. For example, there were moments when I'd be standing alone in the parking lot, soapy water dripping from my brush as I washed car after car; I couldn't help but feel a bit out of place. I'd started to question if I was too far from home to spend my days like this. Feeling stuck in a loop where each day felt like a replay of the last, I wanted something new to happen. It felt like I was at a crossroads, needing a change but not sure where to look.

That's when, out of the blue, I got an email from a former colleague, someone I knew from the small hotel chain I had worked at a few years back. He'd moved up in the world of hospitality and was now suggesting I apply for a role as director of room division and sales and marketing at a 5-star hotel in Bucharest, Romania. The position had been open for a while, but the general manager was struggling to find someone willing to take the plunge, given the country's reputation for being a bit behind the times compared to Western Europe.

Without much thought and even not knowing where Romania was on the map, I decided to take a leap of faith and sent over my CV. Soon after, I said goodbye to the rental car business, packed my bags, and boarded a one-way flight back to Europe. This swift move made me reflect on how life has a funny way of coming full circle. Although I had stepped away from the hospitality industry for a while, my time in Maryland had not only made me fluent in English but also significantly boosted my self-confidence and resilience.

This unexpected chance to move to Romania was like opening a new door back into the hospitality industry, but this time with significant responsibilities and a managerial role at one of the capital's most prestigious hotels. At 26, this was my shot at a fresh start in a field I knew well, armed with new skills and ready to tackle senior operational challenges head-on. It was an exciting turn of events, a chance to step into big shoes as a manager at one of Bucharest's top-notch hotels. At 26, here I was, about to restart my career in a world I was passionate about, and I was more than ready to hit the ground running.

CHAPTER 7
DEFINE YOUR LIFE
GOALS CLEARLY

B ack in 1997, during my final university year, I was juggling studies and a part-time job as a sales manager for three small hotels in Paris. In our downtime, my friends and I often found ourselves deep in conversations about what life had in store for us once we ditched our student hats. Some of my friends imagined throwing big parties to make some money by attracting a steady crowd. Others had aspirations of starting their own music labels. And then, there were those who kept their ambitions a secret, worried someone might steal their big idea.

I would spend a lot of my free time with one particular friend at a café near our university in the Latin quarter of Paris. As we enjoyed our beers, and between sips, we brainstormed about a venture we were excited about selling books and music CDs online. This was quite a novel idea at the time, as more and more people were beginning to explore the internet, either from their home computers or at internet cafés. AOL was a big name in those days, famous for its "You've got mail!" greeting every time you logged in. We were on the edge of a tech revolution, ready to ride the wave, even though the internet crawled at a snail's pace and lacked the sleek browsing tools we have today.

Your biggest concern with starting this online business was figuring out how to buy and store enough books and CDs to meet potential demand. Moreover, people were pretty wary about typing their credit card numbers into a website. Eventually we shelved our grand plan, not knowing that someone in the U.S. was already working on a similar project and would eventually succeed.

This American guy launched an online store named after a legendary band of warrior women. It was a gamble, but some U.S. bankers took the leap, investing in his vision of digital shopping. The company needed a ton of cash for logistics and storage. Fast forward over ten years, it grew into a huge online store, making its founder one of the richest people in the world.

Meanwhile, back in my own world, influenced by the people and environment around me, I began writing personalized letters that I sent out with my CV. I was proud of my achievements in the hotel industry and convinced that an organization would soon see the potential in what I considered a promising career. I believed in my prospects because of my four years of experience, my role as a cluster sales manager, and my Master's degree in Finance from the prestigious University of Sorbonne.

Every week, I would buy a journal with job listings, confident that my profile matched many of the positions advertised. Despite sending out hundreds of letters, I only got a few interviews, mainly with I.T. service companies interested in training new recruits to become programmers in languages like Java, among others. However, these opportunities often required passing advanced math tests, which I struggled with and often failed. They were hunting for engineers, and I just didn't fit the bill. My university education had focused more on economics, finance, and legal studies, similar to a business school curriculum, rather than engineering.

I also recall the time when I, along with several of my university peers, applied for some job openings at a prominent I.T. service company. This particular company had expressed interest in candidates with financial backgrounds similar to ours, which initially seemed promising. However, my personal journey through the application process took an unexpected turn. Unlike one of my friends who managed to secure the position during his first interview despite lacking professional experience, I was rejected.

The primary reason for this was that my four years of experience in the hospitality industry were deemed incompatible with the requirements of the I.T. sector. It was at this juncture that I began to understand the critical importance of tailoring my skills and experiences to align precisely with the specific needs of the company. At that time, I had not yet fully comprehended the necessity of customizing my application to meet the company's expectations exclusively. The company was in search of candidates without professional experience who could be shaped and trained to engage passionately with algorithms.

While on the hunt for a job that resonated with my academic background, I stumbled upon a job listing that appeared to be a perfect match for my qualifications. A few months prior, the small hotel chain where I was employed had been acquired by a leading giant within the French hospitality industry. They were looking for an audit manager for one of their prestigious 5-star properties located south of Paris, which represented an entry-level position within the hotel's finance department. With a diploma in accounting tucked under my Master's in Finance and a shout-out in the job ad for hospitality experience as a bonus, I was sure I was the man for the job.

Consequently, I secured an interview with the hotel's director of finance, and it went smoothly. I did my homework as part of my preparation, arming myself with significant industry insights on the hotel biz, and was ready to engage in discussions that would make a meaningful impact. During this period, the hotel industry in France had begun to focus attention on a new performance metric known as RevPAR. Hence, I was fully prepared to demonstrate my familiarity with this key performance indicator, positioning it as one of the foremost benchmarks for excellence in the hospitality sector.

Throughout our conversation, the director of finance was kind, often pausing to make sure I knew how much he valued my diploma. He also told me there was no need to jump through hoops to prove my worth for the job. It was a breath of fresh air. He shared that the position I was eyeing was still in the planning stages, waiting for the green light from the budget committee. But he promised – as soon as everything was approved, the job would be mine. After sending out so many applications and rarely getting a reply, his promise felt like a warm and welcoming pat on the back, a beacon of hope in the fog of job hunting.

As our interview was drawing to a close, the director leaned in slightly, a spark of curiosity in his eyes, and asked me a question that probably crossed your mind at some point, too: Mr. Savoye, where do you see yourself in the next three to five years?" I paused, not just for dramatic effect, but to really think about it.

When I looked back at him, I was ready with an answer that felt right to me: "I envision stepping into the role of room director or director of sales and marketing at one of your prestigious 5-star hotels abroad."

The director offered a smile, accompanied by a small chuckle, hinting that he found my goals a tad ambitious, perhaps even a stretch. It made sense from his perspective, someone who'd likely climbed the career ladder to his current role over many years.

Now, fast forward three years. Imagine my surprise when I received a call that led me to Bucharest, stepping into the very roles I had dreamt of room director and director of sales and marketing at a beautiful 5-star hotel within the same brand I'd initially applied to for a completely different position. Interestingly, the audit manager position I had initially applied for never came to be, but that application process was crucial. It was my chance to declare my ambitions out loud early on. And astonishingly, those ambitions became a reality much quicker than I had dared to dream, materializing fully within just three years.

Reflecting on this twist of fate three years later, I recognized that what seemed like lofty aspirations at the time had actually transformed into a kind of self-fulfilling prophecy. Back then, I hadn't taken the power of stating my goals as seriously as I do now. I had repeatedly envisioned my career trajectory, imagining leaving my job near Washington DC and foreseeing my return to the U.S., this time aiming for New York City, not for a menial job but for a significant role, perhaps as a sales and marketing director. This specific vision came true precisely three years after my arrival in Bucharest.

And you know what? Years later, when I was ready to leave New York, I had this deep belief that the next chapter of my career would unfold just as I envisioned, propelling me to the position of vice president. And it did, exactly as I had pictured, less than four years after leaving Manhattan.

So, let me share this with you: the power of articulating your ambitions is real. Whether you're just starting out, plotting your next move, or eyeing a leap into something completely new, take a moment to envision that future. Imagine how it would feel to achieve those goals: work hard every day. However, also learn to let go of the tight grip on your expectations. It's a delicate balance of aiming high and trusting the journey. By doing so, you're not just setting goals, as divine forces will help you achieve them. And believe me, you will be surprised by bringing those dreams into reality even sooner than you expect.

CHAPTER 8
GET IDEAS

Feeling excited and doing well in a big project often comes down to having smart ideas and the know-how to make them happen. I truly think that coming up with ideas isn't just about having a high I.Q. or being naturally gifted. It's not something you're just born with or without.

From what I've seen, I get great ideas popping into my head when I'm really focused on solving a specific problem. When I can't stop thinking about an issue, and it keeps coming back to me, that's when a creative process triggers. The constant mental engagement keeps turning the problem over, trying to figure it out, and then, voilà, an idea appears out of nowhere. This can happen anytime, anywhere—even when doing something totally unrelated or in the middle of the night when everywhere is quiet, and the world's hustle and bustle pause so you can hear your thoughts more clearly.

It's like suddenly finding a piece that's been missing from a puzzle right on the floor in front of you, the piece that makes everything fit together. At that moment, you've got to grab onto that brilliant idea and not let it fade away. Don't trick yourself into thinking that it's really good; it'll come back to you later when you have time to think it over. Jump on it right away and see where it might take you. Check if it's something you can actually do. Ideas move fast, and if you wait too long, you might forget it, or someone else might take it.

Another key thing to remember when you've got a good creative thought is not to keep it to yourself but to work with others. By sharing it with the right people, you can come up with a solid plan together. Think about making your idea big, something that can help lots of people. Being able to bring others along with your success is what makes a great leader. It also builds a strong bond with your team, and by showing them, they can make a difference in their work and money matters. People naturally gravitates toward leaders who offer them a way to grow and find purpose in their lives.

When working on your idea with a team, make sure it stays genuine and original to what made it special in the first place. This is what will make it succeed, which is important because people often try to fit new ideas into old boxes. They might unknowingly fall back on what's been done before, even if it didn't work, trying to make the new idea fit with the old ones. This can make the idea feel stale and not as ground-breaking as it could be. Remember, the thrill of something new can be scary, but it's also where the biggest successes come from.

Looking back at the stories I've shared in earlier chapters, I would like to discuss the time when I wanted to start an e-commerce platform for books and CDs during the last year of my Master of Finance. This lightbulb moment came about during my university days at the Sorbonne, brainstorming with close friends about what kind of business we could start using the internet, which was still pretty new back then.

I can't quite remember if it was my friend or me who first mentioned selling books and CDs online, but once it was out there, we couldn't stop talking about it. We realized that selling things online could be way cheaper than opening actual shops. For a couple of hours, we were off to the races, excitedly outlining how the internet could slash distribution costs compared to the traditional brick-and-mortar route. Even though we were excited, we ended up putting the idea aside for a few more rounds of beers instead of really going for it.

When we hit a snag thinking about how to actually get the CDs and books to people, we didn't try to solve it or ask others for help. Moreover, when logistics became a thorn in our side, rather than rolling up our sleeves to find a solution or roping in others who might help, we chose to slip back into our regular routine. We simply dropped the idea and went back to our normal lives, probably to watch some T.V.

Fast forward a few years, when I was driving in Maryland, I heard a radio story about a guy named Jeff who had racked up a huge amount of debt from U.S. banks. He was doing exactly what we had talked about – selling books and CDs online and setting up logistic centers all over the country to do it. It hit me that Jeff was bringing to life the same business we had dreamed up back in our Sorbonne days. Unlike us, Jeff didn't sit around; he was all about making it happen on a big scale.

His financial struggles at that time made me think maybe we weren't so off the mark for not realizing that idea, given the huge financial hole it seemed to have dug for him; at least, that's how it was presented to the whole country. Yet, as the wheels of time turned, my perspective did a 180.

Jeff ended up becoming one of the richest men in the world, all because he took that idea we had and didn't let doubts or the current situation stop him. He didn't even take a decade to turn that idea into reality, fearlessly raising the money needed for those logistic centers without worrying too much about when he'd see a profit. He tackled the Herculean challenge of delivering to customers and all the other hurdles that come with starting something new and turned it into a success story of the 21st century.

When considering this example and comparing it to some of the ideas I've had in my career, while none of them were as earth-shattering as creating online books and CD stores, they've each played a key role in making me successful in sales across different roles. You've seen in previous chapters how I've turned ideas into wins. But you might wonder, why didn't I end up launching a ground-breaking business that could have made me one of the wealthiest people around? Instead, I chose a path that led to great success within my industry.

The answer is pretty straightforward: My focus was shaped by the immediate challenges of my job. Back when I was a student, full of big dreams and eager to make a mark by starting my own business, it felt like there were no boundaries to what I could achieve. Alongside a buddy, we dreamed up a plan to launch an online store. The idea had legs, but somehow, we never made the leap—held back by our tendency to drag our feet and a bit daunted by the sheer amount of work it seemed to require.

Fast forward to my days in the hotel industry, and it's a different story. My world got narrower. I was coming up with ideas left and right related to the business, and with the help of my teams, we made them a reality, turning these concepts into winning strategies. All this happened while I was nestled in the security of jobs that paid well. The contrast between my early aspirations and my later achievements really puts into perspective how the situations we're in and the challenges we perceive can direct how we chase and realize our dreams. In essence, the environment we're in—be it the boundless optimism of our youth or the specific obstacles we face in our careers—plays a huge role in molding the ideas we chase, the risks we take, and the successes we celebrate.

CHAPTER 9
BE RESILIENT

Throughout my career, I've often found myself being eyed as a rival by some pretty intelligent people. I won't lie; the thought that there are only so many roles and chances out there did cross my mind, nudging me to gear up for some healthy competition. Naturally, I figured that outshining others in my field was a straightforward path to achieving my goals and dreams.

But here's where I draw the line—unlike some, I can't remember ever going out of my way to sabotage someone else's success or hatch plans to see them fail, even though I've noticed a few individuals in key positions doing just that. Sometimes, you might find that those higher up the ladder than you aren't exactly on your side, potentially putting your job on the line at critical points in your career journey. In such times, the best you can do is to weather the storm, keep your chin up, and stay positive. Therefore, focus on your work and avoid slipping up; as mistakes could open the door for those with bad intentions to take a swipe at you.

It's baffling, really, why someone would be out to get you, and I wouldn't recommend burning out your brain trying to puzzle out others' dark schemes. Thus, it's far more crucial to keep steering your life toward your goals, especially if a sudden shift in your work atmosphere hints that it might be time to look for new horizons. Always keep your eyes on the prize, remembering that life is full of opportunities.

Indeed, there's a line when it comes to loyalty or pushing forward with a mission in a toxic environment, especially when it risks the well-being and financial security of you and your loved ones. When you sense the winds of change bringing stormy weather, it's more than just a hint; it's a loud call to action. Therefore, seeing the warning signs of a negative shift in your work environment should be your cue to start considering other paths you could take.

Take me, for example. In my late twenties, I was thriving as the director of room, sales & marketing at a 5-star hotel in Bucharest. The hotel was doing great since I was behind the hotel operational delivery, and I had significantly upgraded to provide a real experience of distinguished and discreet service to our guests, not to mention securing several new accounts that boosted our revenue significantly.

Then came Hank, the new regional senior vice president, taking his first tour of our property. I was buzzing with excitement at the chance to showcase what my teams had achieved and to recount our biggest wins in account acquisition to this regional leader. I saw it as a golden opportunity to lay the groundwork for my future career moves. When I first met him, my initial impression wasn't what I had hoped for. Instead of responding positively to my friendly welcome, I sensed a strong negative vibe, as if he harbored some serious reservations or issues with me. This was unexpected and set a tense tone right from the start. A little while later, the hotel's general manager called me for a meeting that seemed like a cross-examination. I was told that I would be watched closely the next day.

Hank stressed the fact that I had to defend my work and have a strong response prepared in case of threat of losing my job. This news was a bolt from the blue for me. I was always enthusiastic about my job and proud of the achievements I had made, despite the fact that I had to compete with a big new player and run a hotel in a less attractive location that needed some renovation.

However, the hotel kept on prospering, and the reason was the loyal customer base I had built and the level of service we offered. To prepare for an anticipated crucial meeting, I chose to wake up at 3 am, go to the office, and create folders containing detailed answers to any question Hank could ask. This preparation included all aspects of our daily operations and strategic reasons for the reorganization of the room division, which had led to a substantial reduction in our staff numbers to increase productivity and efficiency. As a result, I introduced significant salary increases and established new management positions to stimulate professional development and increase employee retention.

This approach was especially successful as it corresponded with the swift economic changes that occurred after the country joined the EU. Paying competitive salaries and providing career development opportunities helped our employees to see a bright future with us or with another company. This method dramatically increased their motivation and productivity at work.

I was about to introduce our new sales strategy, customized to facing the market's changing sands. The town was abuzz with the coming of a leisure segment, and we were all over it. In addition, we caught some big fish – newcomers to the city attracted by the privatization of major, formerly state-owned conglomerates. Our sales organization was quick to adapt, poised to take advantage of these changes and opportunities. I had developed a strong network with the heads of consulting firms that focused on advising big groups that were interested in these state-owned companies.

This network was very useful as these consultants were usually the first to be aware of the major new entrants into the market, which presented a great opportunity for our business. One of my major successes through this strategy was attracting the world's largest steel producer as a key account for our hotel, securing high rates in the process. With a sense of pride in our achievements and still full of energy, I entered the meeting room the next day ready to confront Hank, a man who, despite his chain-smoking habit, could barely hide his clear hostility toward me for the challenging hours that lay ahead.

That morning, I answered every question thrown at me, flipping through the folders I had prepped with care. Yet, instead of smoothing things over, my readiness seemed to crank up

Hank's annoyance. He got so loud his complaints echoed all the way to the lobby, making it clear he was far from happy. It seemed like no matter what I said, it only added fuel to the fire. So I changed tactics, going from talker to listener to what I had to say, and somehow managed to bring our heated meeting to an end. But the day was far from over; Hank had arranged for us to have lunch together, along with my direct reports.

Lunch was, well, awkward. Hank didn't hold back, asking my team directly where they thought things could be improved and how they felt about my leadership. The meal wrapped up with Hank announcing he'd be sending an audit team our way to check if we were all on the up and up with the company's standards. A few weeks later, the auditors came and went, thankfully, without finding any big issues.

A few months passed, and Hank came again for a second visit to the property. However, this time around, his mood had done a complete 180. He was all smiles, praising our achievements. It was a night-and-day difference from our tense first encounters.

Fast forward a couple of years later, and I'm living in Manhattan. Out of the blue, Hank offers me a golden opportunity to move to Prague as the country director of sales and marketing for the Czech Republic. Those years in Prague turned out to be amazing, and Hank became my direct boss and someone to whom I felt genuinely affectionate. We grew pretty close. After plenty of golf weekends and getting to know each other better, I finally felt brave enough to ask him something that had been bugging me for ages. On an elevator ride, I casually said, "Hank, can I ask you something?"

"Of course, Fred. What's on your mind?" he replied, ready to listen.

"You know, back in Bucharest, you were pretty hard on me the first time we met. I've always wondered, why was that?" I tried to keep it light, hoping to make the question less heavy.

He paused for a moment, thinking back, then looked me straight in the eye and said, "Because you are tall."

I thanked him for his honesty and stepped out of the elevator, pondering his words.

It's funny, as a tall person, I've never really thought much about how my height can affect others. That conversation made me realize that something as simple as being tall could have been a source of tension. Friends later told me that my height, together with my confidence, might come off as arrogance to some people. So, what's a tall guy to do? Tone down the confidence I've worked hard to build or try to shrink into the background? It's a weird spot to be in, realizing that something you can't change about yourself could be shaping people's perceptions and interactions in ways you'd never expect.

You will definitely not grow by dodging challenges. We're all about kicking those needless fears to the curb and strutting toward a brighter, more confident future. Think about it – even if you think you're not the sharpest tool in the shed, if you keep moving, you're going to get further than the genius who's just sitting there, thinking about starting. That's a belief I hold dear.

Take my run-in with Hank, for example. At the time, it felt like hitting a rough patch, something we all stumble upon now and then. But looking back, that tough time was a blessing in disguise. A few years down the line, Hank was the one offering me a golden ticket to Prague, turning everything into a fantastic opportunity.

However, as you climb higher on the career ladder, you might bump into some heavier obstacles. There are people out there who wouldn't think twice about pulling the rug from under you, hoping to see you vanish from the professional scene for good. I've taken a close look at some of these characters, trying to figure out what makes them tick. Their game plan? Stay on top by any means necessary, even if it means resorting to gossip, manipulation, or worse, to knock out potential threats.

Why do they do it? Often, it's jealousy or the fear of being overshadowed. They'd rather spend their energy cooking up false stories about high-flyers, hoping to tarnish their reputation and keep their own spot secure. The saying goes, "Throw mud, and some of it will stick." And sadly, it often does. Being the target of such tactics can make your world feel upside down. One day, everything's fine, and the next, it's like you're walking through a minefield with colleagues you once trusted turning against you. Figuring out where this hostility is coming from can be a real head-scratcher.

In my case, I've been in the thick of it, dealing with professional rivals bent on derailing my career. Imagine finding out a colleague is green with envy because you're earning more. They might use any excuse, like company restructuring, to paint you as unnecessary, claiming they can do your job on top of theirs just to avoid being compared to you. It's a tricky situation, but here's the thing – you can't let it get to you. When you realize you've got a target on your back, take a step back, assess the situation, and come back stronger. Remember, the real battle isn't against these detractors; it's about surpassing your own limits and shining brighter than ever before.

And then there are those who might try to pull some strings to get their buddies into your spot, especially if their friend has just lost a job. It's all about who you know for some folks, and they're not concerned about playing that card. There are also the types who won't think twice about making up stories behind your back. They cook up these tales to smear your reputation, maybe even trying to get you kicked out, all because they can't stand the idea of you being seen as the top dog. It's like they can't bear the thought of you shining brighter than them.

Don't be too emotional when you're caught up in situations like this because of those arrows pointing against you. Just understand that it is a sign that someone is working hard to harm you and, consequently, your personal life. It is time to scrutinize the situation, identify where the threat is coming from, and get ready to respond with even more determination.

Sometimes, the best move is to stick it out and prove them wrong. Other times, it might be your cue to look for greener pastures. Remember, when you're facing this kind of pushback, it's often because you're being perceived as a high-value individual who makes others uncomfortable through comparison.

Moreover, pay careful attention to what they're saying about you. If the gossip is just grotesque and doesn't match up with who you are, chances are the persons spreading it are simply projecting their own turpitudes onto you. Creating distance between yourself and such individuals should be seen as a blessing for what is next to come in your life.

Moral of the story? Keep your eyes on your own path. Tune out the chatter and keep building yourself up. Eventually, you'll outshine their attempts to drag you down, showing that their attempts to hold power over you were just smoke and mirrors. At the end of the day, the only person you should be trying to outdo is the person you were yesterday.

CHAPTER 10
COMPETE WITH YOURSELF

I n the previous chapter, we chatted about the bumps in the road you might face while working on climbing up in your career. There are some people out there who, even though they seem to be doing great, will try to trip up anyone they see as competition. They might even try to push out people just because being around them makes them feel bad about themselves.

Here's a piece of advice: Don't get too caught up in getting back at these people. I'm not saying this because I want to sound like the good guy. Going after revenge just sucks up your time and energy. And when you finally think you've gotten revenge, it often doesn't feel as satisfying as you thought it would. You end up just settling a score with someone rather than doing something really great for yourself that you'd actually be proud of.

Build up your skills to be ready for any hurdle that comes your way. This journey isn't just about overcoming obstacles; it's also about creating unforgettable moments with the people who matter most. Imagine having the freedom to enjoy awesome experience with them, visiting stunning places across the globe. That's what exploring this big, beautiful world is all about.

Of course, it's easy to get distracted, maybe by problems at home, temptations that come when you start doing financially well, or just getting too caught up in your own worries. This makes it even more important to stay focused on what you really want out of life. Therefore, deal with any personal stuff that's dragging you down ASAP so you can get back on track to achieving your goals and growing as a person.

I've always believed that real success doesn't come from outdoing someone else or winning at their expense. It's a lesson I've learned over the years, especially when observing the behavior of so-called friends. You know, the ones who are all about sharing in your good times, eyeing your achievements, your wealth, maybe even feeling a bit green over your family life or your partner. They seem to be right there, cheering you on, until things get tough. That's when their true colors come out, and suddenly, they're nowhere to be found. Life's too short to get bogged down by stuff that keeps you from moving forward. Keep your eyes on the prize and stay focused on what you truly want to achieve.

On the work front, I've given plenty of people a leg up, helping them kick-start their careers or climb to that next big rung on the ladder. When they needed someone in their corner to make that jump to a key position, I was there. But when the tables turned, and I hit a rough patch, guess how many of them showed up? Barely any. And don't get me started on social media – it's like they thought hitting the "like" button on one of your posts would cost them something just because it might give your efforts a bit more spotlight.

So, here's what I've figured out about these guys: don't go out of your way for people, expecting something back. Focus on your goals and lend a hand to those who actually add value to your journey. Reflecting on my 30-year working in this field, I can honestly say that the push I got was always from people who had something to gain from helping me. That's why there's no need to feel bad about prioritizing your support. Your main job is to be there for your family, making sure you're doing everything you can to give them and yourself the best life possible.

If others get a lift from being around you while you're charging ahead with your plans, that's a bonus. But be wary of turning into the good Samaritan who gets taken for a ride. My experience taught me that being overly generous doesn't always spark gratitude. Instead, it might just breed entitlement or resentment from those who see your help as just handouts. So, keep your focus sharp, support those who truly matter, and don't sweat the small stuff or the fair-weather friends.

Moreover, it's interesting to see how many people are out there looking for the fast track, trying to skip the hard work by getting into clubs or even secret societies. They think these groups will give them a leg up just because they have agreed to share the same values, even when, deep down, they know it's not the right move. It's like they're drawn to these circles for the things they do behind closed doors, things they wouldn't dare let the world know about, or even actions they can't speak of.

But here's how I see it: chasing after these shortcuts, trying to outdo potential rivals, or looking for backup from groups with iffy motives isn't the way to go. Instead, the real deal, the genuine path to growth, is all about focusing on yourself. There's only one competitor worth beating – and that's the person you were yesterday. Forget about finding the easy way out or mingling with the wrong crowd for a quick boost. Real progress, the kind that sticks and feels rewarding, comes from pushing yourself to be better, bit by bit, every single day. That's where the true challenge lies, not in cutting corners or getting tangled up in shady alliances. Aim to outdo your past self, and you'll find that's the most satisfying victory of all.

Imagine you're trying to be the best version of yourself, who knows how to tackle tough situations and make the most out of free time. Now, think about some choices you have to make: when your gut is pulling you one way, often toward the easy or the fun option, and your head is telling you to take the more challenging path that you know deep down is right, which do you listen to?

When it comes to your job, do you try your hardest and do your very best work? Or are you okay with just doing the minimum needed to get paid, even if it means not really caring about the quality of your work?

And how do you spend your off hours? Do you watch various TV shows or spend your time on hobbies or projects that help you move closer to what you want to achieve in life?

When you wake up early naturally without the alarm, you also have a choice. Do you stay in bed, letting your mind wander aimlessly? Or do you get up and hit the ground running, maybe literally by going for a run? Or do you plan out your goals for the day?

And if staying out late on Saturday makes your Sunday unproductive, is it really worth it? Instead, think about how the best version of yourself would rather ensure that every day counts, including Sunday.

When you're about to decide how to spend the next hour, think about what the best version of yourself would do in that situation and aim to do that. See yourself as a highly efficient person focused on achieving success, not wasting the valuable time you have right now. This better version of you would likely skip over pointless activities and anything that could harm your mind, opting instead to push forward toward your goals. Competing against this version of yourself is worthwhile because, by doing so, you'll quickly become stronger than most people around you and lay down a solid foundation for becoming unstoppable.

Consider dedicating your free time to learning things like sales techniques, working on your mindset, attending social events to build your network, carefully choosing who you spend your time with, and exercising to become both physically and mentally strong. This is the kind of effort you want to put into winning, right?

By adopting this approach, you'll see changes in your life: some people will leave, and new ones will appear; some relationships may end to make room for more significant ones. You'll find yourself where you can seize opportunities because you have the right mindset. When you see the progress of this determined and active lifestyle, it's thrilling to watch the world around you change for the better. You might reflect on people who sabotage others or lose themselves in dubious alliances that could spell trouble in the future. But with a solid foundation based on positive habits and choices, you'll be resilient enough to bounce back without needing help from those who might expect something in return for their support in the past.

Competing against yourself can truly transform your life by encouraging you to step far out of your comfort zone. To make this work; you need to stick with it until these new behaviors are just part of your normal day. One thing you've got to watch out for is the trap of waiting to feel constantly motivated before you start upgrading your habits. It's unrealistic to expect to always be in the perfect mood to get up early for a workout or hit the gym after work, especially if you're attending a social event that day. Since maintaining these efforts requires long-term committing, don't always rely on feeling motivated. Instead, focus on discipline.

Motivation is tied to emotions, which can be fickle. To make lasting changes in your life; it's crucial to establish clear rules for yourself and stick to them. Surprisingly, the benefits, such as increased energy, improved performance, and new opportunities that move you closer to your goals may appear sooner than you think. I will wrap up this chapter with a thought-provoking quote from Harlan Ellison: "Hell on earth would have been meeting the person you could have been."

CHAPTER 11
TOGETHER, WE CAN DO SO MUCH

This chapter describes the skills you need to excel in and establish a solid foundation to help you reach the highest ranks in sales organizations. These skills are the cornerstone of an efficient and effective team that stands out in performance and productivity, ultimately leading to your career growth. Being successful in numerous positions, particularly managerial ones, is reliant on your capacity to build a cohesive team. These teams have to generate outcomes that no one can deny, boost your status within your industry, and attract opportunities that look like a perfect fit with your overall goals.

In the previous chapters, we discussed the basic factors for sales success. This implies practicing specific methods, developing a mindset oriented toward personal development, demonstrating maturity, and strategically placing yourself in managerial positions. The scenario will likely change as you progress in your career, and you may find people around you viewing you as a competitor. However, distinguishing yourself is just about showing that you're the best choice of current leaders for handling problems.

In this case, being the right candidate means you can make a great change for the better. The application of concepts from this book will sooner or later lead you to be chosen over others lacking direction and drive. This should become a straightforward decision for senior leadership if they care about their business. Your clear focus, devotion, and definite goal will be the traits that will make you the top candidate for a management position, setting you apart as someone who is not only aiming for but achieving the highest levels of success around.

As a sales team leader, I focus on maintaining a positive mindset among all team members dedicated to pursuing their own personal success, which will inevitably translate into a better performance of the whole organization. It is important to recognize what really motivates each team member and develop a culture where negativity and cynicism are not accepted. A good atmosphere at work is also required so that each individual can perceive that significant self-advancement is within reach when working with you.

I truly believe that people are motivated to work for and follow a leader when they realize their personal development is also an integral part of their journey with the team. When I think about my job as a leader, it is my duty to show every team member that they could gain a lot from working hard and being part of our success. On other occasions, it might be about helping them to realize that a sales job is more than the perception they may often have initially of the profession, as being the middleman in between a transaction. They can learn faster and grow beyond the expected if they have the proper guidance under your wing.

To actively support the development of sales teams, I recommend providing quality sales training regularly, in addition to reading this book. Indeed, its chapters intend to connect the dots on why going the extra mile in the long run is necessary. It indicates the path to follow for a successful and lucrative career that comes along with roles that become more and more strategic with time.

To enhance your team's development, spark greater engagement, and secure a strong commitment to achieving standout results, empower them with opportunities to expand their horizons. This could imply a culture whereby they could travel frequently to meet with their accounts and their networks, facilitating the provision of funds for client events to let them craft and execute winning concepts and providing them with a platform to shine in front of management, earning recognition both internally and externally.

Twenty years ago, in my position in the Czech Republic, I was in charge of building a sales team from the ground up to represent a big portfolio of hotels. Firstly, I picked out some of those I managed that showed potential. I widened my search by advertising for sales manager position online, and stated that candidates had to have a prior exposure to a sales role.

I went through the applications and selected about 30

resumes, and all these candidates were invited to come in at the same time for an interview. While each one of them had come in expecting a one-on-one interview, they were instead brought to a large room where they were all seated together, each wearing a name tag so that we could take down our thoughts on each applicant during the two-hour session. Three tables were set up for the three assessors, including myself in the middle, facing the audience, ready to guide the group interview we had planned.

The purpose of the process was to simplify it, making it more efficient by filtering out in a short time those who might not fit the team's needs based on their reaction to the group setting and their interaction during the interview. It was also a great way of identifying people who were lacking adaptability, did not have the right open-minded attitude, or were not compatible with the culture I wanted to develop among our own team.

I wasn't looking for perfection but the ability to cope with difficulties and the will to get to the end of the tunnel. I wanted people who could manage the pressure and stay calm under stress, those who could take the roller coaster ride with eyes wide open and enjoy the thrill of a promising job at the end. While giving my speech about the coming selection process and our company, I noticed some people had already left the room, maybe fearing the possibility of going head-to-head with many others. At that moment, a lady from the application list came in late. She gazed around, smiled kindly, and laughed before being asked to take her seat.

That day's method mirrored the one I went through years

ago during the group interview with the US company in Paris. Each applicant had a few minutes to exchange thoughts with a neighbor before sharing with the group why their colleague should be hired. A list of 5-6 candidates were selected after demonstrating their flexibility, positive mindset, promotional skills, and leadership qualities. Lastly, we had an activity in pairs to sell a pen, gauging their questioning techniques.

Next, I conducted a short interview to learn each candidate's background and why they were seeking the position. That day, we picked a new member for our team, which was a win. If we look at the pool of 30 people, the one who impressed the most was the lady who came in late. She was intelligent, adaptable, had a sense of humor, a strong personality, and had persuasive skills. Three years later, she played a key role in the success of my organization when I became the Vice President of Sales for a large portfolio of luxury hotels in Europe. She then got rewarded because she contributed to my success and got appointed as the director of sales and marketing at a prestigious property located by the Danube River in Budapest.

With this recruitment story, I'm trying to emphasize that laying the groundwork for a strong team is crucial, and it should be at the top of the list when you step into a management role. Throughout my career, I've seen many managers stumble in their efforts to build the right team, facing challenges in retaining personnel and often making excuses for failing to achieve results because they lacked a unified and skilled team working toward a common goal.

When faced with a situation where a leader has not managed

to build a team of quality individuals within a few months, and there's no sign that the team and its leader are on track for success, I usually recommend a change in leadership, understanding that sticking with the current setup will only escalate problems without offering a practical solution.

This recruitment journey emphasizes the importance of diligence and the energy needed to select the right candidate. Once she was hired, there was a deliberate effort to train her in sales techniques and equip her with the best tools of that time. Additionally, during her first months on the team, I provided mentorship until she succeeded, allowing her to do the job on autopilot. This time investment in her early stages enabled her to acquire and expand accounts swiftly, eventually becoming a reliable ambassador for the sales culture I was cultivating within my organization.

Years later, it's pretty remarkable when these stellar professionals willingly pack up and leave their countries to work with you again and face the new challenges of your latest position. Watching them significantly boost your success beyond anything you envisioned before showcases the lasting impact of teaming up with such committed colleagues.

CHAPTER 12
CHOOSE STRENGTH AND RISE TOGETHER

In this chapter, we will emphasize the importance of having a strong team and stress the importance of working with people who might even be better than you in certain areas. Achieving success isn't just about assembling a group of individuals but ensuring that they can rapidly grow stronger, leading to more wins for everyone and the whole organization.

In my career, I've bumped into quite a few leaders who seem uneasy about bringing talented people into their circle. It's as if they want to be the star of the show, making every decision because they believe they've got some kind of flawless insight. This usually makes them seem slow to act, lacking fresh ideas, and stuck in a rut. They insist on filtering every new idea through their lens and would often believe that anything that did not come from themselves would most probably be out of interest. This creates a team environment where everyone is more focused on winning the boss's favor than actually thinking independently or coming up with innovative solutions. The primary goal of the team members shifts to not rocking the boat in hopes of eventually securing a tiny raise or a step up the ladder. Leaders like this are keen on keeping everyone unsure of themselves, maintaining an internal image of being infallible or at least uncontested.

You can spot these leaders by how they initially lay it on thick with flattery for people outside their immediate team. But watch closely; you'll see this can quickly flip to using intimidation or cold shoulders if it suits them. They have a toolkit of ways to ensure everyone else falls in line with what they want, or they retreat into their safe zone where they can remain unchallenged. Behind closed doors, they might go on about how everyone else just doesn't get it, convinced they're the only ones holding the ultimate truth.

When you're stuck under a boss who's all about control, planning your exit to better things is vital as soon as possible. Putting up with a leader who's both petty and full of themselves can chip away at your self-respect and stall your career progress—something you definitely want to avoid. To break free, get ahead of the game. Look for chances to shift toward a job that brings you joy, and don't be afraid to take some calculated risks if necessary.

On the other hand, as a leader, I would advise against taking such a pathetic approach to management. Instead, seek strong profiles around you who will speak their minds and provide suggestions. There's wisdom in the saying, "Iron sharpens iron." To grow and climb to the top, open your arms to different opinions and learn to manage strong personalities with finesse.

Creating a workplace culture that values honor, open communication, constructive feedback, and innovative idea-sharing is key for leaders looking to build high-performing teams. Moving away from an authoritarian approach to appreciating diverse perspectives enables leaders to develop teams that are not only successful but also vibrant. Investing in empowering your team members with the right tools and skills can turn them into strong partners ready to tackle future hurdles.

In March 2003, I took on the challenge of leading a major hotel in Manhattan's Times Square. The hotel was struggling, lagging millions in revenue behind its goal. The team felt lost, unsure of how to improve their situation. Just before I started, the sales VP tasked each team member with getting five appointments daily. He figured each meeting should lead to at least 20 overnight stays, which, based on our rates, should help us meet our yearly financial targets.

The hotel's struggles stemmed from Manhattan's downturn after the 9/11 attacks, made worse by the team's lack of deep market understanding—none had received any solid sales training. An authoritarian General Manager made things tougher, failing to spot and nurture potential leads into a successful business.

I quickly realized stepping into this role meant becoming the chief scapegoat for senior leadership, who seemed to be waiting patiently for New York City to bounce back again with significant events and meetings. From day one, I faced strong resistance, especially from the general manager overseeing operations, who was puzzled by the decision to hire someone from Europe who was unfamiliar with the NYC market. I hemmed in by ineffective policies, forcing my team into a frenzy of securing five appointments a day, which often led nowhere due to a rushed approach and unqualified leads.

My best shot at success, boiled down to rallying the team to go above and beyond, even putting in weekend shifts. We all faced the same risk: if we didn't turn the hotel around in six months, we'd probably all get the boot. That meant we had to rely on each other to handle our roles and responsibilities.

In just a few weeks, I needed them to grasp the importance of reaching out to critical potential clients around the hotel. I leaned on the tools I'd mastered to understand the market quickly. I pushed them to lock in five daily meetings with accounts that were not just any leads but ones with real potential. Instead of them going to five small businesses nearby, we shifted focus to big American corporations with branches, travel departments, and corporate travel agencies. These were the real opportunities.

Even though the city wasn't buzzing with big conventions, which usually meant big business for the larger hotels, we still had a huge chance with the corporate crowd. Other hotels around hadn't really bothered much with this segment of clientele before, mostly because it wasn't the big money-maker that tourists were. Plus, our competitors were pretty lost when it came to winning over these corporate accounts; they were too used to a market where the roles were reversed, and it was the customers who were desperate for a room in Manhattan.

What worked in our favor was our hotel's location. We were right where we needed to be, close enough to the headquarters of these big companies, offering an authentic Manhattan vibe that was hard to find elsewhere. The rooms offered breathtaking views of Times Square, making us an excellent choice for guests looking for that awesome New York experience.

Our team was all about accepting the challenge, ready to go the extra mile, and working tirelessly to make sure we nailed this opportunity. We had this team member who really stood out because of his outgoing personality. He had a great sense of humor and a real knack for connecting with people on a personal level. His ability to genuinely empathize with the needs and concerns of others made him super popular with the people who book hotel stays for business travelers. He was so good at winning them over that he became their go-to guy, even preferred over other hotels' contacts.

Impressed by his charm, these bookers often chose an interesting tactic to steer guests our way. They'd tell travelers looking for a luxury stay in Manhattan that those high-end places they used to book were unfortunately full, suggesting they stay at our hotel instead. While not as luxurious, our hotel offered a premium experience that was still top-notch. This clever move filled our hotel with guests. It opened the door to forming new business relationships with several blue-chip accounts, boosting our reputation and success in the competitive Manhattan hotel scene.

This standout team member really took things to the next level. He even got an airline to sponsor flight tickets for important business folks from the West Coast. This way, he could fly them out to New York to enjoy events we hosted on our terrace, which has a great view of Times Square. This initiative wasn't just about impressing them and building strong business relationships. The people who book hotels and these prominent decision-makers loved working with us so much that they started sending more business our way whenever possible.

Then there's John, another key player on our team with his own story. John was only supposed to be with us briefly since he moved to town for his wife's job and was looking for a permanent gig. Even though he was the same age as me, his experience was unique because he came from a strong consulting background. This meant he tackled problems in a very organized and clear-cut way, which was pretty sophisticated. John was ambitious, to say the least, and ready to learn about a new industry without prior knowledge.

He was keen to learn everything from the ground up, especially when using tools that could make our work more efficient. He and I spent countless hours putting together tailor-made pitches for our clients—something quite new and exciting for them, thanks to his experience with big-budget accounts. Together, we came up with a way to find out more about client accounts, offering them something so detailed and compelling that they found our pitches hard to resist.

I showed him the ropes on using insider info to tweak our sales pitches just right. He polished my English until it sparkled, making sure our approach was music to the ears of the big shots we aimed to impress. John picked up sales tricks quicker than a New York minute, and we were a match made in heaven. In under a year, we significantly impacted all the major accounts in town, creating a plan that guaranteed they'd stay with us for the long haul. Once we became preferred vendors in a key city hotel program, we expanded our efforts across the US. Our visits to critical decision-makers and bookers were not just ordinary meetings but high-quality interactions that introduced a new, dynamic way of doing business. This fresh approach was well-received, especially in offices across the US, where we saw a lot of growth potential.

Sure, it wasn't all smooth sailing. We had our share of stormy weather and butted heads more than once, but those clashes turned out to be silver linings, pushing us further. Shortly after I joined, John secured a full-time position, and soon after, he was eager to step up and become my assistant, hoping to take over when I moved on to new challenges. While I appreciated his ambition and recognized his talent, promoting him too soon could upset the team's balance, which I wanted to avoid at all costs. My solution was to prepare him for a more significant role at the corporate level as the director of global accounts, maintaining harmony within the team.

The sales team was thrilled to end 2003 above our budget finally, a tangible proof of our hard work. However, my relationship with the hotel's general manager went downhill, prompting me to look for new opportunities. This search led me back to Europe and the charming city of Prague in the summer of 2004. I made this move despite having the chance to manage a newly renovated luxury hotel in Beverly Hills for the same company. It was a tough decision, but I left with my head held high, having passed those choppy waters and securing well-deserved promotions for two key teammates, sticking to a pact we made months before I left.

Fast forward a few years, and there I was, stepping up as the vice president of sales and marketing for a luxury hotel chain, covering mostly Europe with my base in Luxembourg. It was time to roll up my sleeves and build a small but dream team. Therefore, I chose John for a critical role, and he was more than willing to leave New York City for this new adventure. This choice allowed me to assemble the most effective sales team I've ever worked with, leading ultimately our portfolio to success.

This story underscores the golden rule: picking team members who aren't just flash in the pan but marathon runners, ready for the long haul. However, winning their commitment requires leaders to not only bring them on board but also promote their growth, place them where they can bloom, and make sure they are recognized as an integral part of the team's triumph. As a leader, your playbook should include investing in your team's growth, opening their doors to new opportunities, and ensuring their personal victories are valued as a significant contribution to the team's success. It's about finding the right spot for everyone and turning the team into a well-oiled machine where everyone's contribution is crucial.

Keeping lines of communication open, painting the big picture, and being honest about setbacks all contribute to the formation of a close-knit team. In addition, sharing the vision, the goals, and even the hurdles help everyone feel they're in the same boat, rowing in unison toward a shared destination.

This is the essence of leadership — not just gathering a group of stars but nurturing their commitment, strategically positioning them for success, and steering the ship through calm and stormy seas, turning challenges into stepping stones for remarkable achievements.

CHAPTER 13
RESULTS, NO EXCUSES

In the autumn of 2002, during a sales mission in the US, I had the chance to visit our global sales office, which was impressively located on one of the top floors of the Empire State Building, right in the bustling heart of Manhattan. This visit was particularly memorable because I was introduced to the organization's senior vice president. After our meeting, he suggested I drop by Kirk's office, the vice president of sales. Kirk was effectively the right-hand man of the senior VP and was in charge of driving sales across the entire Americas region.

When I entered Kirk's office, I was immediately taken aback by how clean and organized it was. There was no paper, folder, or pen on his desk, just a laptop. Kirk, a man in his 40s with a noticeable bright and metallic gaze, welcomed me with a sly smile. He gestured for me to come closer, indicating he wanted to share something on his screen with me.

I quickly recognized the data on his laptop screen. It was a detailed city sales report I had analyzed for years as head of sales in Bucharest. With Kirk's permission, I leaned in to get a better look at the screen. I began to point out various data points, recognizing our hotels' potential market share opportunities based on the performance metrics of different companies and sources of business shown on the screen.

Kirk seemed genuinely interested in my analysis. After a brief but insightful discussion that lasted less than five minutes, he politely ended our meeting. As I was leaving, he casually thanked me and wished me well. Later that day, to my surprise, I received a call from the senior vice president offering me the leadership position for the sales department of their flagship property on Broadway in Times Square.

Just a few months into my New York adventure under Kirk's wing, it was like being strapped into a high-speed roller coaster. I was tasked with turning around a hotel already trailing behind its financial targets by millions. With his eagle eyes, Kirk was all over us because our performance weighed down the entire US company's results. And Kirk was in a league of his own as a salesperson, no doubt about it. He was a former Navy SEAL who had somehow morphed into a sales titan. How he made that leap was beyond my understanding, but he was hands down the most formidable salesperson I'd ever encountered.

Kirk's confidence was unshakeable, standing firm against any shadow of doubt like an impenetrable fortress. His speech, rich with military jargon, made it clear he was no ordinary business leader but a tactician who viewed the sales world through the lens of combat. In his eyes, the team was a platoon, each member equipped and ready for the sales frontline. The possibility of "casualties" or setbacks didn't bother him; his eyes were fixed on victory, and any sacrifice along the way was deemed necessary. The last thing I wanted was to be tagged as MIA (missing in action), a fate Kirk ominously hinted at for those who didn't meet objectives. His rule was ironclad: failure to hit targets was unacceptable, and issues within the team demanded immediate action, preferably without needing his direct intervention if you wanted to limit the magnitude of damages that would inevitably follow.

"Results, no excuses" was Kirk's ultimate principle, spoken with a mix of resolve and a slight edge of contempt for failure. This brutal but effective management style and constant high-pressure conditions forged my sales and management skills in the fire. Without this rigorous challenge, I wouldn't have reached the level of sales expertise I possess today.

Years later, reflecting on these days, the stress and relentless demands under Kirk's leadership left a lasting imprint. Yet, this very experience became the bedrock for developing my own management approach and establishing a resilient, bulletproof sales culture. It shows how important it is to keep to work on strengthening the sales mindset among your team members.

Therefore, focusing on building and always boosting a sales culture in your team is key to success. By clarifying what's expected regarding leadership approach and performance, such a sales mindset will make everyone feel connected. It builds pride and brings out the best in each person, helping every team member discover their potential.

But it's not all about hitting numbers. A strong sales culture fosters a genuine sense of pride and responsibility. It's the kind that lights a fire under each team member, compelling them to use their skills to the fullest, find innovative solutions, and make meaningful contributions. Imagine a team where each member is clear about their role and feels genuinely proud to be part of it. This isn't about doing just enough to get by; it's about being part of a bigger picture, where grit and gumption are the secret sources to overcoming hurdles and clinching success.

Having been in the trenches with sales teams from the ground floor to the executive suite, I've learned the importance of clear communication and shared goals. By conducting detailed business reviews, delivering stirring speeches at sales conventions, and providing hands-on training, the concepts from this book can be turned into standards, empowering team members, and establishing clear expectations for their performance. Consequently, with the right mindset and readiness, they will be well-prepared for standout performance.

This approach is all about making sure the whole team is aligned, on an individual basis, on their personal interest of reaching our targets as a team. By following the advice in this book, team members not only help the company succeed but also get to earn more money, get promotions, and go through a journey toward becoming much stronger.

Therefore, mentorship plays a crucial role in steering individuals toward productivity, leading to professional achievements and positive changes in their personal lives in just a few months. They quickly become skilled in creating opportunities, honing their persuasion abilities, and mastering sales techniques rooted in a deep psychological understanding of others. As their confidence surges, success fuels further success, bringing not only rewards within the organization but also earning the satisfaction and respect of business partners.

Hence, the emphasis is on creativity, urging individuals to come up with bold ideas. This sets off a positive cycle, making it clear to leaders that these innovators are vital for success and often lead them to leadership roles. As they get better at mastering these creative and technical skills, they naturally begin to mentor their teammates, building a robust group of sales professionals focused on their growth and the organization's success.

There are some smart routines in place to keep our leaders on their toes, like weekly one-on-one catch-ups and regular sales meetings. These gatherings are the perfect time to share results, discuss challenges, successes, brainstorm, and answer any questions that need clarification. Therefore, leaders are encouraged to be understanding with their teams, but by this point, they should know that with the right mix of skills, the knack for spotting opportunities, the grit to keep going, and the drive to push through, there really isn't any room for not meeting goals, tackling problems, rallying the team, or getting new initiatives off the ground. Hence, each team member is expected to raise their sales game, making success inevitable.

Also, the sales culture I've developed over time is guided by a simple rule inspired by Kirk, often summed up in those three words: "Results, no excuses." This approach, shaped by years of experience, moves my team's mindset away from making excuses to a strong determination to meet our goals. Once the team really gets this idea, they start thinking more about solving problems. They focus on using what they have effectively and making decisions that put them in a great position to succeed on time.

However, if someone isn't fully committed or doesn't take their role seriously, they won't be seen as a leader by their team and will likely stumble often. They'll shy away from the risks they need to take, failing to motivate or involve their team effectively. This inability to move forward in a competitive market will likely lead to the team's downfall. That's why I use this simple formula to evaluate a new leader: If there aren't visible results within three months, they might not be the standout leader I expected. If there's no improvement after six months, I start questioning their leadership ability. And if a year goes by without any notable achievement, it's time to think about bringing in new leadership.

I always end up saying that the tough decisions we make aren't personal. It's all about how the business needs to run. I mean, hanging around in a situation that's going nowhere? That's not an option. Every leader has this one big job: ensure the core business stuff is ticking over nicely. If a sales leader isn't on top of that, it's not just their problem—it starts to mess with everyone, all over the place. And let's be real, that's a situation we just can't let slide.

I've seen it time and again, most leaders, they get it. Once they really understand how serious things are, they step up. They make the necessary changes so we don't end up in that tight spot. Only a few find themselves in a pickle, kind of lost and tangled up in problems they should've sorted out way before they ever thought about leading a team here.

CHAPTER 14
VISUALIZE IT

Here we are at the last chapter, and we're starting with a powerful piece of advice from Novak Djokovic himself. After winning at Wimbledon, he shared what makes him successful, not only in tennis but in life:

"Whatever you are pursuing in the world, whether it's tennis or anything else, you know, I was a 7-year-old dreaming that I could win Wimbledon and become No. 1 in the world one day. So, one thing is for sure: I feel that I have the power to create my own destiny. I try to visualize every single thing in my life, not only believe it, but really feel it with every cell in my body, and I just want to send a message out there to every young person: be in the present moment. Forget about what happened in the past; the future is something that is just going to happen, but if you want a better future, you create it. Take the means in your hands, believe it, create it."

— *Novak Djokovic, a professional tennis player, is 2023 ranked world No. 1 in singles by the ATP*

Therefore, this book has laid out strategies for you to follow, highlighting the importance of staying strong and focused even during the darkest times when life tests each of us. Mastering these skills can propel you to the top of your game in sales or any career path, really, as long as you know, in detail, what you're aiming for.

In my own journey, I've always had some kind of a premonition about where I was headed next, and more often than not, it turned out to be right. Just like the old saying that faith can move mountains, some early 20th-century thinkers believed in the power of the laws of attraction in the unseen quantum world. They argued that if you can picture something clearly in your mind and think about it often, you have the power to bring it to life in the physical world.

If such a paradigm exists, there's something to be said for keeping that kind of thinking in your toolkit. Imagine your goals vividly, plan out your path, and make choices that steer you in that direction. Djokovic himself talks about the power of visualization, about really feeling the emotions and satisfaction of achieving his goals before they even happen. Setting clear goals and diligently working toward them is paramount for using your time efficiently and achieving a fulfilling career and life. It's about crafting a career and a life that's rewarding. And at the heart of it all is a belief in your own abilities to reach your desired destinations.

Let me take you back to what would lead to a turning point in my career during the winter of 2011 when I was in charge of a luxury hotel portfolio in Egypt for a reputed European player.

It seemed like a straightforward challenge, given how many opportunities were out there. But then, everything changed on January 25th, when a revolution started, the Arab Spring. Suddenly, the usual sales channels to activate tanked, and we had to think fast, switching to online sales, particularly for our Cairo spot. Despite all the challenges, this move actually worked wonders, and our Cairo hotel started outperforming all the others along the Nile for months.

Nevertheless, because of the escalating political unrest in Cairo, with increased insecurity, rioters on every corner, and a curfew that snuffed out the vibrant nightlife, it became painfully clear I needed to leave Egypt. The city's harm, so alive before the revolution, was now overshadowed by turmoil. Just when the situation seemed most dire, I received an unexpected offer to apply for a job at one of the world's largest hotel groups based out of Vienna.

This job interview was a career opportunity and a chance to escape the chaos enveloping my life in Cairo. Returning to Vienna, a city I had visited many times before while living in Central Europe, I discovered it anew. Vienna revealed itself in a different light this time, casting a spell on me with its winter beauty. The streets, adorned for the season, made the city appear more magnificent than ever, offering a serene and stunning contrast to the unrest I was eager to leave behind.

I went for an interview for a regional director of sales role, and I'm feeling pretty good about how it went. Missing out on this job meant I'd be stuck in Cairo's chaos without a backup plan. Walking through Vienna's streets, taking in the winter air, and watching people chill in bars made me realize what I was missing. But then, back in Cairo, I got the let-down of my life: they picked someone else instead. There I was, back to square one, needing all the positivity I could muster to find another way out.

Commuting daily to my office in Cairo took about an hour by taxi, so I got into reading. One book, "The Power of Your Subconscious Mind" by Dr. Joseph Murphy, really caught my attention. It conveyed its ideas with a scientific approach, suggesting that if you intensely imagine a desired situation and genuinely feel the emotions connected to that scenario, your subconscious will begin working to make it happen. So, with my memories of Vienna vivid in my mind, I started to envision myself there every day, driving a BMW, in an effort to bring back those good vibes.

Then, a few months later, out of the blue, I received an unexpected call from Kirk, an old acquaintance from my days in the US who now resides in London. He suggested I apply for a job at the company he worked for, which is a big name in the hospitality industry with thousands of hotels worldwide. This was the same company I had previously applied to for a sales role. He told me about an opening for a senior director digital role in London, so I quickly submitted my application online.

A few weeks later, I was in London for my final interview, this time with the company's president responsible for revenue and distribution. I focused on highlighting the digital skills I had honed since my time in Egypt. The interview felt positive, and I flew back to Cairo that same evening, hopeful. A few days later, Kirk called with an update. He started with, "Fred, it went well during your interview, but…" My heart dropped, thinking I had missed again the opportunity. Then he surprised me by saying the president had plenty of candidates for the senior digital role but was struggling to find someone suitable for a different position. This role was to oversee revenue for Central, Eastern Europe, and Turkey, and I was the top choice for it. Kirk asked if I would consider switching to this new role.

Feeling a wave of relief, I quickly told Kirk, "Yes, of course! But will I be working near London?" Kirk's reply was even better, "Yes, you could be based there, but there's also the option to work from Vienna since the operational vice president is there." You can probably guess which city I ended up choosing.

Arriving in Vienna, hoping to stay longer this time, I was thrilled when given the choice to lease a car – between a Mercedes and a BMW. My choice? The BMW, without a second thought! This turn of events proved to me how powerful visualization can be. Just months after setting my sights on Vienna, I found myself working in this dream city, but through an unexpected path with the same company. This experience is a reminder to me of the endless possibilities that lie ahead, boosting my confidence and reinforcing the belief that we can indeed become who we aspire to be.

As we wrap up this book, think about the huge number of opportunities out there waiting for you. Picture what you want your future to look like and start working toward it, step by step. Remember, sales aren't just about being good at selling things. It's about transforming challenges into stepping stones and moving closer to your dreams by making strong connections with people, leading effectively, and being brave enough to try new things.

Yet, on this path to undeniable success, you'll face challenges and obstacles. There might be moments when you feel stuck or unable to connect with the right people. During these times, when doubt creeps in, you should pause. Take a moment to look around, breathe in your surroundings, and find strength in the quiet assurance of your own inner voice, encouraging you with a gentle yet powerful reminder: "Raise your sales game!"

About the Author

Frederic Savoye has an extensive career spanning three decades, where he's led sales and commercial, teams at big international corporations, particularly in the hotel and leisure sectors. He's worked across the globe, including the US, Europe, and the Middle East, and is recognized for his innovative and result-driven approach to sales.

What sets Savoye apart is how he combines a positive mindset with advanced sales techniques and leadership strategies, leading to significant success. He has shared these methods with many professionals, helping them climb to the top of their careers.

Frederic Savoye has recently moved into the field of asset management, focusing on big projects in the Middle East. In this new role, he uses his extensive experience in sales and leadership but in a different setting. By working on these projects, Savoye shows how skills in sales and leadership, acquired during his journey across the globe, can be applied to help develop and manage large teams in charge of major projects. His career path encourages and inspires others to look beyond their current roles and explore how they can develop and use their talent in new and more creative ways.

YOUR FEEDBACK MATTERS TO ME

I really appreciate you taking the time to read my book. I value the time you've spent with it, and your interest means a lot to me.

If this book struck a chord with you and added something meaningful to your reading collection, I'd be incredibly thankful if you could share your feedback. A quick review on the platform where you bought the book would be fantastic.

Your feedback is more than just your thoughts; it will help me understand what works for you and how I can improve my future books.

I'm all ears for what you have to say—which parts you loved, what caught your attention, and any suggestions you have. Thanks again for being a part of this adventure. Your insights are truly invaluable to me.

Made in the USA
Monee, IL
10 August 2024

be601104-d592-4fee-b44d-08f6a82cb3dcR02